Spain's Cause Was Mine

SPAIN'S CAUSE WAS MINE

A Memoir
of an
American
Medic
in the
Spanish
Civil War

Hank Rubin

Foreword by Peter N. Carroll

To Scott

Hank Rubin

Southern Illinois University Press
Carbondale and Edwardsville

Library of Congress Cataloging-in-Publication Data

Rubin, Hank.

    Spain's cause was mine : a memoir of an American medic in the Spanish Civil War /
Hank Rubin.

       p.   cm.

    Includes index.

    1. Rubin, Hank. 2. Spain—History—Civil War, 1936–1939—Participation, American.
3. Spain—History—Civil War, 1936–1939—Personal narratives, American. 4. Spain—
History—Civil War, 1936–1939—Medical care. 5. Spain. Ejército Popular de la República.
Brigada Internacional, XV—Biography. 6. Americans—Spain—History—20th century.
I. Title.

DP269.47.A46R8   1997

946.0817—dc21   97-15733

ISBN 0-8093-2159-9 (cloth : alk. paper)   CIP

To Lillian

My Comrade, My Love

And So That

Marci, My Daughter and Blake, My Grandson

May Know

They gave up everything, their loves, their countries, home and fortune; fathers, mothers, wives, brothers, sisters and children, and they came and told us: We are here. Your cause, Spain's cause, is ours . . .

—*Dolores Ibarruri,*
"La Pasionaria," 1938

Contents

Illustrations

Hank Rubin, 1937, in his clinical laboratory at the
base hospital in Valls, Spain   *Frontispiece*

Following page 34

Hank Rubin, as a child, with his father, Benjamin W. Rubin,
and sister Audrey

Fannye Rubin (Rubin's mother) with her family, the Seeligs

Courtyard of the base hospital, Valls, Spain, 1937

Granville Walker Paine, age 22, 1937, one of Rubin's
comrades who was killed in Spain

Ministerio de Defensa Nacional's authorization
of Hank Rubin's departure from Spain, November 27, 1938

Hank Rubin, 1939, newly returned from Spain

Hank Rubin during World War II, Brisbane, Australia, 1944

Hank Rubin, 1996

Foreword

For college students sixty years ago, no less than today, the choices of the day sometimes boiled down to simple decisions, such as to "blow my almost empty wallet on a hamburger for lunch," as one UCLA undergraduate put it, or, as his lab partner replied, to "go into the library and do the research for Dr. Webb's paper."

So much for appearances. On an April day during the spring semester of 1937, Hank Rubin chose to do neither. And then, just a few minutes later, while sunbathing on the steps of the UCLA library, another student came along with a better proposition: How would you like to go to war in Spain?

"Sure."

Reading the plain and honest recounting of this conversation, one is tempted to seek psychological understanding: the young man's conflicts with his father; the fear of failure during the nation's economic depression; ambivalence about his Jewish heritage; a bad love life. There is plenty of grist in this narrative for speculation.

But psychology is not the point—or the methodology. When Hank Rubin replied "Sure" and embarked on the road that would take him to Spain as a volunteer in the International Brigades fighting to save the legally elected Republic from its fascist enemies, he was participating in a worldwide political movement that attracted college students and alumni from every corner of the United States, not to mention men from innumerable occupations, economic backgrounds, and educational attainments. In Spain, the North Americans were assigned to the 15th Brigade, and initially called themselves the Abraham Lincoln Battalion. As more volunteers arrived, they formed a George Washington Battalion and then the Mackenzie-Papineau Battalion, named after two nineteenth-century Canadian patriots and ostensibly composed of Canadian recruits. Many U.S. volunteers served in the "Mac-Paps," which is where Hank Rubin was first assigned.

Exact numbers are difficult to establish. Contemporaries estimated that forty thousand volunteers from fifty-four countries served in the Brigades. Of these, about twenty-eight hundred came from the United States— from every state except Delaware and Wyoming. The median age was twenty-eight; statistical "modes"—the ages with the most volunteers—were twenty-three and twenty-five. So Hank Rubin, at age twenty-two, was younger than most. He was certainly more educated than most. And unlike most military recruits, he was able to use his academic training to specific advantage in Spain.

Besides the men who volunteered for military service, some 150 North American doctors, nurses, and medical technicians also enlisted in the ranks. Hank Rubin's recollections of work in hospital laboratories is especially valuable because the Spanish Civil War proved a testing ground not only for weapons of war but also for military medicine used during World War II. It was in Spain, for example, that the Canadian doctor Norman Bethune developed techniques for preserving blood that made possible indirect front-line transfusions. Nor were medical personnel spared the hardships or the dangers of war. Two U.S. physicians were killed during bombings, and one nurse was severely wounded. Indeed, ambulance drivers learned to remove medical insignia from their vehicles because fascist pilots seemed to be drawn to such targets. And while the medical staff was well trained in civilian medicine, the shortage of personnel, hospital equipment, and even food placed all patients at risk.

Especially significant is the extent of Hank Rubin's duties. The fact that a UCLA undergraduate was given so much medical responsibility and so little training underscores the severe shortages facing the embattled Republic. When General Francisco Franco's military rebellion erupted in July 1936, Spain's civilian workers and loyal militia, women no less than men, confronted the insurrection and succeeded in defeating the disloyal army in many cities. But within days of the outbreak of fighting, Nazi Germany under Adolf Hitler and fascist Italy under Benito Mussolini began sending military assistance—planes, supplies, and troops—to support the rebellion. Both England and France, worried that hostilities would spread through Europe, hoped to isolate the Spanish war by adopting a policy of nonintervention and ordering an embargo on all military shipments to Spain. Germany and Italy formally accepted the policy and subsequently participated in international meetings to avow compliance. But neither fascist nation paid any attention to nonintervention, blatantly violating the agreement. In April 1937, Nazi air forces of the Condor Legion bombed the Basque town of Guernica, immortalized in Picasso's painting; the same pilots later flew missions over Poland at the beginning of World War II.

Despite the hypocrisy of nonintervention, U.S. policy under Franklin D. Roosevelt followed the lead of Britain and France. After 1937, U.S. passports bore the stamp "Not Valid For Travel In Spain." In that age of isolationism, the willingness of volunteers like Hank Rubin to defy federal law illuminates the deep political passions of the times. While leaders of the so-called "western democracies" adopted strategies of appeasement toward the fascist peril, many informed citizens well understood that another world war loomed ahead, unless international aggression could be stopped. Hank Rubin's quick decision on the library steps reflected less the impetuosity of youth than it did the sound realization, sadly proved prophetic, that Hitler meant to embroil Europe in war. Letters written home from Spain by Lincoln Brigaders repeated that refrain endlessly: If fascism isn't stopped in Spain, another world war, including the United States, was imminent.

While Britain, France, and the United States agonized about implementing nonintervention, the Soviet Union had no illusions about doing business with the fascist powers. Aware of German and Italian involvement in Spain, Josef Stalin and the Communist International began to extend aid to the Republic late in the summer of 1936. The first International Brigade volunteers arrived in Madrid in November, participating in the dramatic defense of the city. The first U.S. recruits sailed from New York the day after Christmas. The organization of the Brigades—from enlistment to passage—remained under Communist party supervision. Yet among the Lincoln volunteers, the percentage of communists (members of the party or the Young Communist League) remained about 70 percent, and some of those had joined a communist organization in order to get to Spain.

As Hank Rubin's memoir attests, the recommendation of a party member was the surest way of enlisting. (The failure of the Socialist party to field a "Debs Column" showed the difficulty of handling such a complicated international operation.) Once in Spain, however, communist soldiers enjoyed no special privileges. Non-communists served as officers, even occasionally as political commissars, providing educational and morale assistance to the soldiers. Yet all U.S. volunteers, regardless of their political beliefs, were later treated as communists by the U.S. government—labeled "premature anti-fascists" by the military during World War II and blocked from the rank of officer, tailed by the FBI and various state agencies, and placed on the attorney general's list of subversive organizations in 1947—twice, in fact: as the Abraham Lincoln Brigade and as the Veterans of the Abraham Lincoln Brigade.

Hank Rubin's ideological leanings also reflected his ethnic background. Most Lincoln volunteers, born just before World War I, came from urban areas with high immigrant populations. About one-third, maybe more, were Jews, though seldom orthodox. Given the international orientation of immigrant families and the obvious Nazi threat, the high participation of Jewish volunteers might be expected. Sketchy evidence from other countries suggests that Jewish refugees from Germany and central Europe appeared in disproportionate numbers. Among medical volunteers, Yiddish often served as the common language in hospitals.

Yet, as befitting a group of second-generation Americans, ethnic issues remained muted in favor of assimilation. The eighty-some African Americans were well integrated in the ranks; the Lincoln Battalion commander Oliver Law was the first to lead a racially mixed army in U.S. history. There were also half a dozen Native Americans, two Chinese Americans, and one Japanese American, as well as representatives of almost every white ethnic group. This self-conscious melting pot ideology dovetailed with the politics of the communist "Popular Front." Recognizing the importance of a common anti-fascist movement, radicals set aside factional and sectarian differences to affirm their shared commitment. In 1936, the head of the U.S. Communist party could assert that "Communism is twentieth-century Americanism."

Such ideological posturing too often obscured the genuine sentiments that motivated volunteers in the Spanish Civil War. Whatever their political affiliations, ethnic backgrounds, economic circumstances, or educational accomplishments, Lincoln volunteers understood the issues, the stakes, the danger. They went to Spain anyway. "They gave up everything," declared Dolores Ibarruri, "La Pasionaria" of the Republic, at the farewell ceremonies in 1938, "their loves, their countries, home and fortune; fathers, mothers, wives, brothers, sisters and children, and they came and told us: We are here. Your cause, Spain's cause, is ours—it is the cause of all advanced and progressive mankind." As she spoke, Spanish women threw flowers at the volunteers' feet and broke into their lines with hugs and kisses; battle-hardened soldiers wept openly. "You can go proudly," she told them. "You are history. You are legend."

Unlike Hank Rubin, nearly eight hundred U.S. volunteers could not go home at the end of the war. Of them, wrote Ernest Hemingway, "no men ever entered earth more honorably than those who died in Spain." Those who did survive could never forget the loss of their comrades. Although many proceeded to follow successful careers—Hank Rubin as a restaurateur, wine columnist, and teacher—Spain remained the central ingredient of their lives. During the long nightmare of the Franco dictatorship, Lincoln veterans agonized over the cost of their defeat. But after Franco's death in 1975, Spain moved peacefully toward a republican government. And in 1996, to mark the sixtieth anniversary of the outbreak of the war, the Spanish government offered a token of thanks by granting the rights of citizenship to all the surviving veterans. Now more than eighty years old, Hank Rubin could claim that honor in return for his youthful commitment.

—Peter N. Carroll

Acknowledgments

Thanks and appreciation to Betsy Amster, Bob Cantor, Peter Carroll, Scott Clemens, Steve Gomez, and Dorothy Jones for reading the manuscript.

And to Milt Wolff, who kept my chronology of battles straight.

Most of all, to my wife, Lillian, who read the manuscript in its various stages, making suggestions and offering criticism, and who encouraged me every step of the way.

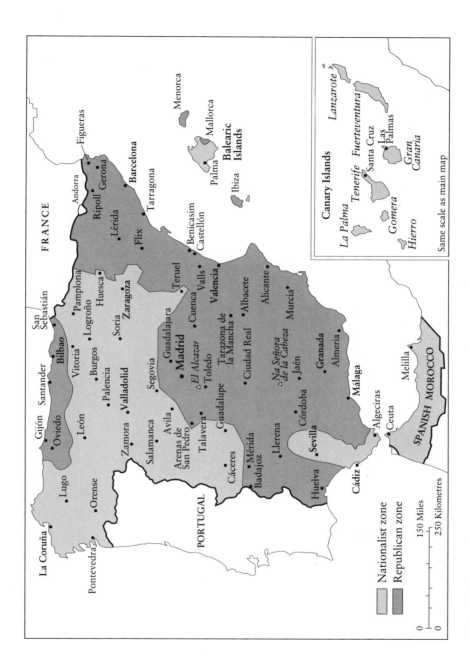

A divided Spain, July 1936

Nationalist zone
Republican zone

0 150 Miles
0 250 Kilometres

Canary Islands

Lanzarote
La Palma Tenerife Fuerteventura
Santa Cruz
Las Palmas
Gomera Gran Canaria
Hierro

Same scale as main map

FRANCE

Figueras
Andorra
Ripoll
Gerona
Barcelona
Lérida
Flix
Tarragona
San Sebastián
Pamplona
Huesca
Logroño
Zaragoza
Soria
Teruel
Cuenca Valls
Valencia
Benicasim
Castellón
Bilbao
Vitoria
Burgos
Palencia
Guadalajara
Madrid
Albacete
Alicante
Murcia
Santander
Gijón
Oviedo
León
Valladolid
Segovia
△El Alcazar
Toledo
Tarazona de
la Mancha
Ciudad Real
△Na Señora
de la Cabeza
Jaén
Granada
Almería
La Coruña
Lugo
Zamora
Salamanca
Avila
Arenas de
San Pedro
Talavera
Guadalupe
Cáceres
Mérida
Badajoz
Llerena
Sevilla
Córdoba
Málaga
Algeciras
Ceuta
Melilla
Huelva
Cádiz
Pontevedra
Orense
PORTUGAL
SPANISH MOROCCO

Menorca
Mallorca
Palma
Ibiza
**Balearic
Islands**

Spain's Cause Was Mine

CHAPTER
1

UCLA

It was noon. I was standing on the quad of the University of California at Los Angeles near the entrance to the library, trying to decide whether to do the research for a paper for my parasitology course or to walk down to the Student Union cafe and blow my almost-empty wallet on a hamburger.

Dave, my lab partner, came by and tried to coax me to join him.

"Let's go into the library and do the research for Dr. Webb's paper. We can split the work and do it in a third of the time."

"I don't trust your arithmetic. Even with the two of us we'll still be stuck there for hours. Maybe longer."

Dave put his hand on my shoulder.

"Hank, if we do it together it'll be so much easier."

Only slightly guiltily I joked, "Hey, at the moment the mating habits of the tsetse fly on some tributary of the Upper Nile don't excite me. I really don't feel like working. It's too nice out here."

"Come on, Hank, I have to cut out to go to the dentist for a three o'clock appointment, so I can't do it later."

Half turning my back to him, I replied, "I just don't feel like it now, Dave. I just want to sit here and enjoy myself. Anyway, I have an idea for revising the fifth chapter of my novel that I want to think about.

"For Christsake you're a premed. Quit dreaming about being a writer and get off your ass."

"I know, I know, but I'm going to sit here for a while."

"You're a hell of a partner and a lazy bum," he growled and left.

I sat down onto the red brick steps of the library, leaned back and soaked up that beautiful April day with the sun on my face and my mind roaming free. I was filled with a sense of serene well-being. Thoughts of reports were far away. Life was pleasant and nothing urgent seemed to push on me.

Suddenly I was aware of someone standing before me, disturbing my daydreams. I looked up to see Rep, a slim, blond-haired student whom I knew only vaguely as the campus Red. He sat down on the steps next to me, leaned back for a while, and then, in a whispered voice that sounded as if he were trying to sell me filthy postcards, he asked, "Hank, how would you like to go to Spain and fight with the International Brigades against Franco?"

My startled but not antagonistic look prompted him to go further. "I must tell you that the casualties are very high . . . about 50 percent mortality, and a high percentage of the survivors are wounded."

A real truth-in-advertising approach!

It was April of 1937 and the Revolt of the Generals in Spain was eight months old. Spain, a small country at the bottom of Europe, had not been an important factor in international politics for many centuries. Another armed revolt there ordinarily would not have attracted much more than passing attention in the United States. Therefore, the press and radio devoted relatively little space or time to it at first.

But the extensive introduction of a large number of troops and massive amounts of armaments from Hitler and Mussolini to the side of Franco had made it a matter of international interest and concern. A Non-Intervention Pact pledging all member nations not to give military help to either side was passed by the League of Nations. That focused world attention, and media coverage expanded and became continuous. All of a sudden, the war began to seem as if it could spread outside Spain. Newscasters and writers were even speaking of the possibility of its becoming another world war.

A Gallup poll in 1937 showed that two-thirds of the people in the United States were unconcerned about the revolt. This reflected, among other things, a high point in isolationist feeling in our country. Of those who expressed any concern, twice as many were for the Republic as were for the rebels. (A year later a combination of the growing distaste for fascism in Europe and the popular support for the American volunteers saw the proportion of the population who were unconcerned drop from two-thirds to forty percent. Of those who took a stand, three-quarters were pro-Loyalists.)

The expressions of those who chose sides were very intense. The battle cry of the Madrileños, *No Pasaran* ("They shall not pass"), became a common cry among the liberal/left student body, and the expression was almost a password among us. Indeed, it spread to the rest of the campus and was the rallying cry used at football games when our team was defending its goal line.

Inside Spain there was a bitter conflict between the government and the hierarchy of the Catholic Church, which, until the advent of the Republic had been the official religion of the country. Church officials and most of the priests totally sided with Franco, but the overwhelming majority of their congregants favored the legal government. This intense division between church and state had its strong reflection among Catholics in the United States. Here, as in Spain, many rank-and-file Catholics sided with the Republican government. But the Catholic leadership made a strong and vocal commitment to the revolt, giving it their blessing and pressuring President Roosevelt and the Congress to support the side of the insurgents, or, at the very least, to remain neutral.

While in some ways the war seemed very far away from the UCLA campus, meetings of both the pacifist and the antiwar movements were filled with heated discussions about it. We couldn't escape the questions raised by the Revolt of the Generals. Could the cause of the Republic be so righteous and the danger of fascism so real that the Spanish government merited support? Was the threat of communist control, of which the Republic was accused, so serious, so real, that armed rebellion was justified?

Heating our discussions were reports coming out of Europe of the action by the fascists against Jews and Catholics. In Germany, Jews were forbidden to use swimming pools and beaches. Catholics were arrested when they didn't incorporate pro-Nazi words into the celebration of the Mass. The Nuremberg Laws of 1935 had stripped the Jews of their citizenship. The reactionary nature of both Hitler and Mussolini became something we talked and argued about. A German ship, the SS *Bremen*, had docked in New York flying the swastika, and in a dramatic move, a group of New York seamen had torn the flag down just as the ship was preparing to return home. This well-publicized action intensified anti-Nazi awareness and feelings in the country.

Stories of Americans who were volunteering for the International Brigades to fight on the Republic's side, many from college campuses around the country although none from our school, made it sound romantic—so much so that I had speculated about what it would be like to go. We didn't hear about the horrors those volunteers faced in actual fighting. What came through was a picture of young men fighting a glamorous "good fight" without any idea of what battle really meant.

As I considered Rep's proposal, I remember thinking, with the arrogance of youth, "But of course I'd be in the half that survives." It wasn't merely a thought, it was as if I had been picked up by the scruff of the neck like a kitten and physically moved from the side of the killed to the side of the survivors. I don't mean that going off to fight was an idea free of anxiety. Even youthful arrogance and heroic fantasies could not make war that safe in my mind. I knew I could be wounded, but in my imagination it was a wound that I could bear with stoicism, much as a badge of honor. And after being hit in the heat of battle I would, of course, continue firing my gun bravely at the enemy, defending and saving our threatened position. Thus did my mind bring my fear under control, mute it to the point where it could be pushed aside.

With such thoughts of heroism capturing my imagination, with hardly a pause to reflect, I shocked both myself, and Rep, by saying "Sure."

Startled, he looked at me for a moment. "Are you really sure? This is no joke. It's serious business."

I looked at him, threw my shoulders back, and said, "Of course I'm sure. That's what I said."

"Wonderful! That's wonderful, Hank. That's a fine and proud decision."

He paused for a moment and then began speaking slowly, with emphasis, his eyes never wavering from mine as he spoke to me.

"But there are rules. Very important ones. This is a secret decision on your part. No one! No one, not your parents, your best friend, your girlfriend, no one can know. If word gets out the FBI will clamp down on you. You'll probably be kicked out of school. You won't be able to get a passport. I know that not sharing this may be the toughest part of all, because I can't tell you when you'll leave—possibly it won't be for a couple of months. We don't have exact schedules. It takes planning to get you there. We just have to wait until word comes from the East. And you'll be sitting here in Los Angeles all cranked up to go and you can't leave. Yet your lips must be sealed.

"Is this clear? You really have to understand this or everything will blow up in our faces. In a very real way from this moment on you're under army discipline. Do you think you can keep your mouth shut?"

"Yes, I can and will."

Rep continued. "It also means that you have to keep out of all demonstrations, picket lines, open political meetings. Not only that, no drunk driving, no speeding tickets, no getting drunk, because if you do get drunk you'll probably blab. You aren't Catholic so I don't have to tell you not to go to confession, but you can't go to a rabbi to talk about it. Your folks can't know."

"I'm an atheist, and my parents would be the last I'd tell."

"If you have to talk, then I am the only one you'll have to talk to, no one else. No one."

I nodded my head once again.

While I nodded my head like a good soldier, inside I was thinking: Not getting drunk wouldn't be easy but not too hard. Not being political could be done without stress. Keeping my folks out of it would be no problem, especially my Dad. But not telling anyone? Not sharing this momentous news with my closest friends? My girlfriend? That seemed almost impossible. A cloak and dagger routine would be fun. I could see myself as the mysterious political soldier. But not telling anyone? Not getting the approval I knew they would give? Not being able to get my due as a political hero? That was going to be hard. Very hard.

So why did I say yes?

I can't give a clear and rational answer, something definitive. How much was youthful impulse, bravado? How much a feeling of a moral responsibility to society? How much because I was Jewish? These reasons were there, and much more. There were so many factors that, as I think back to more than a half century ago, the best that I can do is to tell a little about the world in which I lived, about who I was, and about my dreams.

The year was 1937, the middle of the Great Depression. Poverty, fear, unemployment, and demoralization were widespread: The lines of the unemployed seemed endless; wages were falling for those who continued to work; every day more businesses went bankrupt; factories were being abandoned; there were a stream of families spreading out from the failed farms of the Midwest Dust Bowl to other states, usually heading west to California. When men were able to keep their jobs, it often meant that their wages were cut. It was the time about which John Steinbeck later wrote in *The Grapes of Wrath*. Among the youth there was a sense of alienation from the establishment, for we had nowhere to go, little hope of meaningful jobs, or, if we were employed, little chance for security or advancement.

But coinciding with these painful conditions was a need to fight back to make our world more tolerable, more livable. This resistance was expressed in political ferment that showed its face daily all over the country. John L. Lewis formed the CIO (Congress of Industrial Organizations), which in twenty months grew to more than three million members, two-thirds of them organized in a union for the first time. These new industrial unions in steel, auto, rubber, and the oil industries, organized on an un-heard-of scale, challenged both industry and the old-line craft unions of the American Federation of Labor. Massive sit-down strikes in the auto industry were, in large part, successful. Longshoremen led a huge general strike that spread from the waterfront to the whole city of San Francisco and shook the establishment to its core. The Maritime Union on the West Coast grew in strength and militancy.

These worker actions and movements grew out of the conviction that taking almost any action was better than accepting conditions as they were. The desperate circumstances that pushed them into action and the early victories formed the background against which there was a growing feel-ing of strength, a feeling that workers could organize, demonstrate, strike—that they could succeed in making their lives better. Farmers, particularly those in the Midwest, often banded together at farm foreclosure auctions to forcibly block the federal marshals. One of a group of neighbors would bid one dollar to buy back a neighbor's foreclosed lands and homes. Oth-ers armed with guns or pitchforks would surround and threaten anyone who looked like he might make a higher offer.

There was a sense abroad that the world, or at the very least our na-tion, could be different, that there could be less pain, less poverty. The defeat of Herbert Hoover and the election of Franklin Delano Roosevelt, with all his shortcomings, had brought with it a feeling of hope, of possi-bility.

My family, while not homeless or penniless, had been hit hard by the depressed economy. In Portland my father had been the Northwest re-gional manager for the Missouri State Life Insurance Company, the thir-teenth-largest life insurer in the country. Then, suddenly, the company went under, one of only three insurance companies in the United States to go bankrupt during the Depression. Until that moment his earnings had been large enough to place us in the very comfortable upper-middle class.

With the company's failure, Dad not only was out of a job but, in addition, the overwhelming portion of his savings, which had been in-vested in company stock, became worthless. The insurance policies he had bought on his own life, as well as those he had sold to his clients, were assumed by another company, but the price of that bailout was that each

Missouri State policy was socked with an extra 50 percent on its annual premium. Some policyholders who could not pay the extra premium had their insurance canceled. Those who could pay the extra amount were angry at Dad for selling them a policy with such a financially precarious company. With his reputation tarnished, my father felt he could no longer sell insurance in the Portland area. Suddenly he had no job or income or client base. Ashamed, he decided to leave Portland and move to Los Angeles, where his parents lived. There, over fifty years old, he would have to start all over again.

The shock of leaving the city where I was born, the neighborhood that I had been a part of, was disruptive to my plans, my sense of belonging. My expectation of going to the University of Oregon in Eugene, where I had already been interviewed for membership by a fraternity, was left behind. I was angry about the events that had disrupted my life, but I also felt a surge of inner excitement about my totally new future. My plan to go away to college, which few of my friends were able to do, had already started a separation process for me that made the idea of leaving my home less hurtful. What it meant for Mother and Dad to leave all their friends, to leave their financial and emotional base, was something I gave little thought to; my primary feelings were a mixture of anger at being displaced, balanced against the excitement of a new home, new friends, a new school.

The folks sent me ahead to southern California to live with some family friends while they sold our home and liquidated their remaining assets. During these months I attended Pasadena Junior College. A half-year later, when they came south, we moved to Los Angeles into the upper floor of a duplex in the Wilshire district near La Brea, a middle-class area of the city. My maternal grandmother, then in her late eighties, came to live with us.

A rough financial period followed, a period during which we lived in a sort of genteel poverty. What money we had came from digging into the capital from the sale of the Portland house and some little help from my grandfather, who then lived about a mile from us. Dad went back into the insurance business, but during the first year or so he worked out of the house and sold only a very occasional policy. For each of the few policies sold there was intense competition, because many of the retirees in southern California had turned to selling insurance to make ends meet. Most people were lucky just to be able to survive in the present; protecting the future with an insurance policy wasn't an option.

At my new home, I transferred from Pasadena City College to Los Angeles City College, which was just a fifteen-minute streetcar ride away. Because our family had a car and we paid more for rent than was allowed for those receiving public assistance, I was not eligible for government aid from the National Youth Administration. But I was able to get a job in the Bacteriology Department of the college where I was taking courses. It was a wonderful fit for me, and I began to think seriously of switching from a premedical to a bacteriology major. I was so enthusiastic about what I was doing that I spent most of my spare time in the lab and was soon made chief assistant.

At the end of my sophomore year I had to transfer to UCLA because LACC was only a two-year school. Taking the bus to the campus in Westwood required walking almost a mile to catch one, and most days I hitchhiked my way to and from the campus. In those days people were not afraid to give rides, and to thumb one's way was often faster than taking the bus.

Even though school fees were minimal, I had to work to pay them. My job was also my source of spending money. My steady work was as an assistant in the experimental zoology lab. That didn't seem like drudgery because it opened new ideas in science for me, and I made friends with upperclassmen who were doing projects for their classes or working for their advanced degrees. A couple of times a week I spent the evening waiting on tables and washing dishes at fraternity and sorority houses, taking a regular route from one to the next. I found the fraternity members snobbish, and I learned to hate fraternities. But many of the sorority members flirted with me, and that was fun.

After a bit I scraped together twenty dollars and bought a second-hand 1924 Chevrolet sedan, the running expenses for which I could manage by taking fellow students to campus. My fees undercut the bus fare, and, because I was able to park on campus and drop my passengers off near their classrooms, my service was attractive and I had no trouble keeping the car full. Then one day the transmission dropped out in the middle of the street, and I went back to hitchhiking.

Once I'd overcome my anger at having to move from Portland and having to make new friends, the Depression didn't seem so bad to me personally, mainly because most of the students who were my friends were in the same boat. Being in school, all of us were somehow making it in much the same way. Looking back now, I realize that my folks kept most of their money concerns from me. It was not that I was unaware of what was going on in the world. There was no escaping the terrible things that were happening in the country, for that was front-page news. But neither I nor my friends were really suffering. If we didn't eat steak every day, we certainly weren't hungry or victims of malnutrition.

There was no money for new clothes, but I got around that by creating my own fashion. Rain or shine, winter or summer, I wore white cotton ducks and a white, short-sleeved, cotton knit shirt that buttoned at the throat. I could keep my clothes neat and clean in the washing machine at home. The outfit was outrageous enough that I soon earned the nickname the "white pagoda."

Mother brought a few dollars into the family coffers by taking orders from acquaintances for cakes or other of her specialties, such as candied orange or grapefruit peel. Having an excellent reputation as a cook and baker, she didn't have to do much solicitation. My job was to do the delivering, which I wouldn't have minded—for I got to use the family car—except that I was always sent out with the admonition to be sure to wait for the money. I felt that the orders to Mom were a gift because we were poor, and the collection of money seemed demeaning and embarrassing. I was always shamefaced to ask for the money, feeling as if I were a beggar.

While I was attending UCLA, the everyday and demanding realities of my premed studies began to hold less interest for me than the draft of the novel I was trying to write, the pages and pages of poetry that came flowing from my pen, or the music I listened to on the radio or at concerts. The idea of being a doctor and curing illness had been a part of my dreams since I was ten or eleven, a goal that grew, as much as anything, from my contact with my brother-in-law, who was a doctor and who had become a role model for me. But by the time I signed on to go to Spain, I was having a hard time finding the discipline necessary to achieve that goal. I wanted to be a doctor, but I was increasingly pulled in other directions—to write, to paint, to make music. In addition, the turmoil in our nation—the political world in which I lived, the emerging crisis in Europe, and the revolt in Spain—engaged my emotional interest in ways that my classes and labs could not.

One of the questions that always puzzled me was why Rep had chosen me—a non-communist, not distinguished in school politics, athletics, or anything else. I knew that those he asked must be a limited, rather select group. I was pleased and flattered by his attention, by the fact that he considered me capable of doing the job, mature enough to be responsible, and a person with ideals. But I couldn't figure out why. Was it because I was a member of the leftist American Student Union, or because I was Jewish and a large percentage of the volunteers were Jewish? I didn't think to ask him then, and I never found out the answer.

In the personal, internal realm, the reasons for my going started with the fact that I was less than two months short of twenty-one, young, healthy, and full of energy, with my hormones surging and probably out of balance. Or as we would have put it then, "full of piss and vinegar." The sense of adventure was surely a factor. I had no serious commitment to a woman at that time, so there were no emotional or sexual ties holding me back. I was still a virgin, and my sexual turbulence was high.

Perhaps, too, because our culture has no rite of passage, no way to mark the transition into becoming a man, I had a strong need to prove myself. While the Jewish religion has its bar mitzvah at the age of thirteen as a passage into adulthood, that ceremony was something I had done as a matter of course, "for the family," without a great deal of personal meaning. My focus for the ceremony was on not forgetting what I was supposed to say or mispronouncing the Hebrew words and phrases that I had memorized. It didn't make me feel grown up, and I wasn't given any new status or adult privileges as a result. I don't suppose that any thirteen-year-old really feels like an adult.

Going to war seemed to me a step into manhood. I must confess that the imagery of personal heroism that accompanies soldiers in wartime appealed to me very much. It would be a heroic gesture that would be almost as good as composing a great symphony, painting a masterpiece, or writing the great American novel. My fantasy life had always been filled with the grand gesture. But in real life I didn't know who I was, even who I wanted to be. Even my plan to be a doctor didn't mean that I thought of having a routine practice. Rather, I dreamed of discovering the cure to some horrible disease or creating some great new surgical procedure. At the moment when I was about to embark for war, however, I was more closely identified with being a novelist than a doctor. The romance and heroism of going off to a war that Ernest Hemingway and Ralph Bates were already writing about touched my novelist's soul. What better way to get the depth of experience, the real understanding, that would enrich my writing? And also to be a heroic figure at the same time?

Although my politics definitely leaned leftward, I was politically unattached. I subscribed to no political theory and belonged to no party or organization other than the very progressive American Student Union, although I also attended meetings of the campus Zionist Club. I doubt if I could have articulated a coherent reason why I chose that organization instead of another liberal student group. Perhaps it was as simple as the fact that a friend had asked me to join. Once I did, however, I stayed because I liked the political direction of the discussions at its meetings and, as well, the people I came to know there.

Complicating the political climate on campus was a pacifist movement centered around the Oxford Pledge, originating from Oxford University in England, which was a pledge not to volunteer for any military service and to be a conscientious objector to all wars. But pacifism struck no resonance within me. Turning the other cheek is not my style. More attractive to me was the antiwar movement—that is, opposition to our country's involvement in any unjust war, such as a war of oppression or conquest. Opposition to war held considerable attraction for me, because of the stories out of World War I that told of the pointless cruelty war brought to civilians, the introduction of poisonous gas, and the mass tragedy that that war had created. This blood-stained history from two decades earlier was being kept alive by motion pictures and novels.

Many of my friends were active in one or both movements, but their arguments against war often sounded much the same. If our country were bombed or invaded, for instance, I could not conceive of taking a pacifist stance, of not fighting, for example, against an urgent, direct threat of fascism. So, although I was involved in the discussions and the arguing, I couldn't find a comfortable place to land with either group.

The decision to go into combat seems all the more strange to me when I think of my basically noncombative personality. My tendency is to avoid conflict, to be a peacemaker, to try to find a face-saving way out of a confrontation for all concerned. Part of that noncombativeness was reflected in an automatic siding with the underdog in almost any situation. The fact that I saw the Republic in that role elicited my strong sympathy, partly because I felt myself to be an underdog.

As a young boy, before puberty, I had been short and fat. That meant being teased by my classmates and, equally painful, always being last chosen for a team. Later, no longer short and fat, reaching an even six feet and weighing about 160 pounds, I still was not much of an athlete. Although I had considerable strength and endurance and lots of energy, it was not combined with much speed, physical skill, or agility. In a culture in which athletes were heroes and their exploits defined manliness, I felt as if I had been passed over when such gifts were handed out. Even in my family, where athletics were not an important measuring stick, my father teased me unmercifully about being ungraceful and awkward. When I ran, he laughed and described it as "galumping." "Henry, you are as graceful as that bird known as the elephant," he taunted repeatedly. I hated it, and I hated the cruelty of those words. Yet so desperate was I for his love and approval that when I was a little boy I'd sometimes run with an even more pronounced "galump," hoping to make him laugh, so that maybe that would make him love me.

The fact that I was Jewish and had grown up in Portland, Oregon, which at that time still had a strong Ku Klux Klan presence, was another important part of my motivation. In the 1920s, there were still some KKK signs around the city, and one of the large banks was known as the KKK bank; many of its officers were acknowledged members of the Klan. Not many Jews lived in the city at that time, and fewer still were in the schools I attended. I don't mean that I encountered much overt prejudice or discrimination at school, but Jews were not elected to class offices. And there was always a sense of "outsiderness."

I was angered that so many Jews had let themselves be annihilated or degraded in czarist Russia without fighting back. My father and his family had not fought back but had left the Ukraine and moved to this country. And the news coming out of Germany indicated that the same thing was happening to Jews once again.

The neighborhood celebrations of Christmas and Easter reminded me that I was not quite a part of the community, of our block, or of my school. In grammar school, when we had to report in class what we had done to celebrate the Christmas holidays, I never knew what to say. Walter, next door, told of the bike and the sweater he had received. Robert, across the street, related a family gathering, a wonderful meal, and presents. If I spoke of a Chanukah celebration, they looked at me as an odd curiosity. My neighbors were kind, but nevertheless, they had a way of putting me in a special category, apart from them.

Of the volunteers to Spain from the United States, about 30 percent were Jewish, with the proportion among medical personnel as high as 62 percent of the surgeons/physicians, 75 percent of the oral surgeons, and 58 percent of the nurses. For most of us religion was not a primary motivation, although Jewishness was an important factor. I later found out, when in Spain, that most of my Jewish comrades, like me, were atheists, or at the very least agnostics. But Jewish historical experience makes us especially sensitive to oppression anywhere, and it is moreover a moral requirement of Judaism to fight against injustice and inhumanity.

One of the strongest influences operating on me at the time was my relationship with my father. In my middle to late teens I was in a very active and very unpleasant separation struggle. Struggling for my independence, I hated him and wanted to get out of the house. I didn't want to have to accept anything from him or be dependent upon him. Yet, despite all of these antagonisms, I also had a strong sense of family and a deep attachment to my mother.

In so many respects, Dad was a very strong negative role model. His sense of family line and the Rubin name, most particularly his name, was almost an obsession. Since in his mind the succession was only through the male line, his focus was on my carrying on the family name. What he wanted most was for me to join him in his Los Angeles insurance agency, eventually taking over and perpetuating the firm name of Benjamin W. Rubin and Associates—making it "Benjamin W. Rubin and Son." That I had set my scholastic goal on being a doctor was about as much as he could possibly stomach.

He was a lifelong Republican—an affiliation that held no attraction for me, since it represented standpattism, resistance to change, the hopelessness personified by President Hoover, and a heavy tilt toward the rich. But even if I had agreed with his politics in that moment of my active separation struggle, I would have been unable to accept his values. His conservatism and my antipathy to almost anything he stood for pushed me further along the path to the left on which I had already embarked. The way he laid down the law in the house, how he dictated what my mother might or might not do, his unwillingness to accept any of my struggles for identity, were part of what I hated (and still do).

I had nothing but disdain for his hypocrisy of decrying anti-Semitism and then in the next breath railing in a racist way against blacks. I believe that this was my first ideological conflict with him, back when I was only twelve or thirteen. A still-vivid memory is that first time I challenged this contradiction during a dinnertime conversation. He was telling mother about a business meeting he had had that day at which one of the participants was blaming everything on the Jews. He described how mad he had been and how impotent he felt, because he was trying to sell the man some insurance and felt he could not speak out. A moment later, Dad started to talk disparagingly about the blacks in much the same vein that his potential client had attacked Jews.

"Dad, why do you talk about how the Jews are talked about and then talk in the same way about the blacks?" I fearfully asked. "That doesn't make sense to me, and it doesn't seem fair."

"Henry, you don't understand. You just don't know what you are talking about. It's two different things. Blacks are different." Then he snapped, "Mind your manners. And don't you dare be disrespectful to me."

There was no arguing with him. His word in the house was law.

But my movement leftward was also motivated by my search for something to believe in, a system of ethics and morality and a way of life that I could honor. I knew that a society that suffered from wars, unemployment, and poverty as well as racial, religious, and sexual discrimination needed change. But just what that meant or how we might bring that change about was still unknown to me. The image of the United States as a melting pot that would boil down to form a single nation of Americans seemed right to me. The idea of Jewish separateness, centered in a unique country such as Palestine, was just unacceptable. While keenly aware of anti-Semitism in the United States, I did not know or, perhaps, want to know or want to believe how deep-rooted and vicious the practice of anti-Semitism was in other countries, how widespread it was, or even to what degree it existed in my own country.

In these pre–World War II years, the Left seemed to be the only segment of our political culture that was as worried as I was about fascism. The new order in Germany and Italy frightened and angered me. The demonstrations and radio broadcasts of our own homegrown, would-be fascist leaders and organizations—such as Father Coughlin, Gerald L. K. Smith, the Silver Shirts, the Ku Klux Klan, the Christian Front, America First, the Black Legion, the Nazi Bund, the Vigilante Corps, and the Secret Army—did not give me any confidence that dictatorship and overt anti-Semitism could not come to this country. In Los Angeles we heard reports that members of the German-American Bund were beating up Jews on the streets of New York. The echo of storm troopers' boots reverberated across an ocean and a continent to stir my fears.

As a Jew and as an American, I felt a responsibility to fight against anti-Semitism and fascism. Going to Spain seemed a way to strike at Hitler and Mussolini and, at the same time, their counterparts in this country. My anxieties about anti-Semitism and its relationship to the war in Spain were fanned by the comments of Quiepo de Llano (known as "the radio general"), who was one of the four generals who started the rebellion against the Republic of Spain. In one broadcast he said that theirs was "a war of western civilization against the Jews of the world." The German press said such things as "The Spanish Republic was a Jewish communist attempt to conquer Europe for Bolshevism." Cardinal Isidro Goma, archbishop of Toledo and primate of all Spain, broadcast to the defenders of the Alcatraz that they were defending against "the bastard soul of the sons of Moscow . . . the Jews and Freemasons . . . the dark societies controlled by the Semite International." And one of the slogans of Nationalist fund-raising was "He is a Jew who hides his gold when the Fatherland needs it." The Franco government had printed a cheap edition of the violently anti-Semitic tract "The Protocols of the Elders of Zion," which was distributed widely.

My parents had always been members of a synagogue, although hardly active in their religious practice, and I was brought up as a Jew. However, since the age of twelve or thirteen I had been a committed atheist, completely denying the existence of God. And I was a very assimilated Jew— perhaps even one who was afflicted with the kind of self-hate that anti-Semitism breeds.

One evening early in May, shortly before leaving for Spain, I attended a meeting of the campus Zionist club at a friend's home because I was interested in that night's discussion. It was about Biro-Bidjan. Because the Zionist movement was then finding serious resonance in Russia, the pressure for an exodus from the Soviet Union was growing in strength. Stalin's counterproposal was that the Jews of Russia move to Biro-Bidjan and form another of the many autonomous Soviet republics. At that moment it seemed a good idea to me.

I spoke up. "Why not," I asked, "go where the government sponsors a homeland, rather than fighting for space in a desert where we aren't wanted and which will surely mean lethal conflict with the Arabs living there? I don't know much about the Palestinians, but I am sure there will be lots of fights all the time and people on both sides will get killed. What difference do the biblical myths about location make?"

My suggestion met with unanimous opposition. I was a minority of one.

Part of me enjoyed being the dissenter, the freethinker. But in some deeper part I was uncomfortable, feeling lonely and isolated, a reminder once again that wherever I went I seemed to be, if not quite an outsider, not quite a full member. After the meeting was over and all of those attending had left, the discussion leader of the evening asked the hostess if I was a member of the Young Communist League, apparently because I had sounded its theme. The next day when we met on campus, the hostess told me what the speaker had said and with an icy stare asked, "Are you?" I didn't know how to answer her hostility. Until that moment I had thought of her as a close friend, someone who shared my questions and doubts about our society, someone who was open to all kinds of ideas. Finally I stammered something incoherent and left, feeling the sadness of knowing that I had misjudged a friend, perhaps even had lost one.

During this period, the Communist party and its program was out in the open. It concerned itself with jobs, trade unions, care of the dispossessed, the elderly, and racism. Socialism was its eventual goal, but that seemed something to be achieved in the distant future, almost pie-in-the-sky. For the present the party turned its attention to the immediate problems stemming from the Depression, the problems that were the ones that seemed important to me. The program was so broad that by 1936 much of the presidential platform of the Communist party had been adopted by the Democratic party, and four years later some of its planks, such as Social Security, were also in the Republican party platform.

The communist slogan, "From each according to his ability and to each according to his needs," sounded more rational, more kind, and more like the philosophy of a society I could respect. The reality of the Soviet Union, the complex ideology of Marx, and the actual practices of Stalin hardly made a dent in my consciousness. All I knew was that the Communist party at that time was the leader in the struggle for change, for the things I wanted for our country. And I particularly appreciated the party position in support of the Spanish Republic. Most of all I needed some structure on which to hang my emerging political ideals. That exchange with my friend, and the whole incident of the night before, forced me to do some serious rethinking. The more I did, the more it seemed to me that if I sounded like a communist, then I probably should be one. Obviously the decision was not taken simply because I had spoken the party line on one issue, at one meeting. While I was vague on what socialism was in practice, the idea of the communist movement and what the party was fighting for beckoned me.

On my twenty-first birthday, in May, already committed to fight in Spain, I decided to join the party. No one recruited me. In fact, I had to look up the address in the phone book and take a streetcar to the drab, downtown Los Angeles office that was the headquarters for both the Los Angeles County Communist Party and the Young Communist League. There I explained that I wanted to join the YCL. Jack, the YCL official I met with, was more than cautious in our interview. He questioned me at length. Both the party and the Young Communists were justifiably nervous about assorted spies and FBI agents seeking to infiltrate the organization. Jack hemmed and hawed for a long time, slipping in challenging questions every once in a while. Finally, he asked who would recommend me for membership. Since I couldn't think who might certify me as politically safe, for I knew only a couple of campus YCLers, and those only casually, in desperation I gave him the name of Rep. It was the magic bullet that broke his reserve. All of a sudden he knew who I was, for apparently Rep had kept him posted. I was accepted and enrolled.

Now smiling in friendship and comradeship, Jack recorded me as an at-large member, not a member in the UCLA club. "For security you won't be enrolled in a club until you come back. You are not to go to meetings, in fact don't be visibly political. No one is to know about your volunteering." Then he carefully made out a membership card, signed it, handed it to me for inspection, and finally, as a security precaution, took it back. He would hold it until my return from Spain.

All of my personal and social reasons coalesced at that moment. Yet the decision to go had had little to do with Spain itself, about which I knew almost nothing. And what little I did know, I disliked. Although it had been the vanguard of civilization in the Middle Ages, the Inquisition in the mid-fifteenth century, in which the Catholic Church and government had showed its great intolerance in its treatment of the Jews, was, of course, loathsome to me. Those Spanish Jews who had converted to Catholicism but were accused of lapsing in their conversion had been treated brutally, many being burned at the stake. Those who didn't convert were expelled from the country.

The conquest of America by Cortez and others had seemed heroic when I first learned about it in grade school. But then as I began to understand the brutal treatment of the native population, my admiration had faded. The bullfights, synonymous with Spain, which I knew from movies and books, were another sort of violence that was repugnant to me. And the power of Spain's royal family offended my sense of democracy and fairness. All of this seemed to indicate a country of blood and violence.

Was this the country I was suddenly willing to die for?

But modern Spain, the country I was planning to fight for, had changed. Neither communist nor socialist, it was a country in transition that stood in the center of the fight against fascism. The Republic had come into being just a few years earlier, in 1931. In place of rule by oppression and brutal political power, Spain's government had passed from being an oligarchy controlled by the rich and powerful to being a republic of the moderate left, which meant the most reformist section of the organized working class, the socialists, the petty bourgeoisie, and the Republicans. For the first time, religious freedom was national policy. State financial support for the clergy and religious orders was eliminated, and the religious hierarchy was stripped of its secular power. Orders such as the Jesuits, which swore allegiance to the Vatican, were dissolved. With the coming of the Republic, the people were using many of the churches and cathedrals for hospitals and assembly halls. Trade unions were legalized and encouraged. Democratic changes were also made in the army. Eight thousand military officers who refused to swear an oath of allegiance to the government were retired (albeit on full pay). The armed forces lost jurisdiction over civilians and no longer could arrest anyone simply because a member of the military felt that a civilian had insulted the army.

But if the political power had shifted, the economic power had not, and those holding that power were united with the church and the army. The power elite regarded any attempt at reform as an aggressive challenge to their historical privilege and attacked all reform measures.

While the new government was struggling to find a new concept of rule, the Republic was in serious economic straits. By 1933 there was 12 percent unemployment overall, and in the southern, agricultural part of the country that figure was nearer 20 percent. Part of the problem was internal. But the worldwide depression intensified such problems and left little hope for outside help. The elections of 1933, two years after the establishment of the Republic, saw a shift to the right. This victory was a signal to the power elite to retaliate for the meager gains the workers had made in the first two years of the Republic. Wages were cut, jobs eliminated, rents raised, and renters evicted. Many landowners let their holdings go idle, which resulted in their farm tenants being without a livelihood. The period between 1934 and 1936 was one of bitter polarization, and was labeled as *El Bienio Negro,* the black biennial.

Political strife was intense. Alcalá Zamora, the prime minister, unable to form a stable alliance of the Right, dissolved the Cortes (parliament) on January 4th of 1936 and called for new elections to be held on February 16th. In the election campaign, the Right formed an alliance called the National Front of the CEDA (Catholic party), the Falange (fascists), the Carlists (traditionalists/monarchists), the Agrarians, and the Independents. The Center had trouble uniting and ran a weak campaign. The focus of the attack from the National Front was against the Center, which meant they discounted the strength of the Left. But when the votes were counted, a popular front of left-wing Republicans, the Republican Union party, the Socialists, the Communists, and the Catalan Separatists had won with 278 Cortes members. The National Front had only 134, and the Center 55. Even an alliance of the Center and Right would relegate them to a minority status.

The Left's victory touched off a whole series of events: The government granted amnesty to all political prisoners. A series of agrarian reforms settled between fifty and one hundred thousand peasants on their own land before the end of March. Employers who had let employees go had to take them back and indemnify them for lost wages. At the same time, however, the value of the peseta fell sharply, and leading financiers began to send their wealth out of the country.

From the time the election results were published, civil unrest, along with violence, arson, and murder, became widespread. Some who were released from prison violently expressed their rage at having been imprisoned. More often, it was the Falangists who wanted to discredit the government by increasing disorder. In this way they would justify a "regime of order." In spite of this disintegration, there was a euphoria on the Left. Unfortunately, the two major trade unions and the left-wing political parties were fighting among themselves, and this intensified the disorder and prevented the government they supported from acting decisively on almost any front.

When the Republic came into being, back in 1931, a plot had been initiated by the leaders of the army, the monarchists, and the clergy to overthrow it. But when the government of Prime Minister Zamora did not take any decisive action against the liberal forces, the plan had been put on hold. With the Left's electoral victory, the plot was once more activated.

While Spain was caught up in turmoil, other European countries were moving toward dictatorship and fascism. Apart from Germany and Italy, Salazar was in command of Portugal; in Poland the fascist legions of General Pilsudski had overthrown the republic headed by Paderewski; Metaxis had created a dictatorship in Greece; in France the Cagoulards and the Croix de Feu were shouting for the blood of Jews, trade unionists, members of the Frente Popular, and Freemasons; and England had a very conservative government.

Through May and June everything in my life felt like it was on hold. The time seemed endless, for I was not permitted to share this new phase in my life with anyone. That was the hardest part—not being able to share, to brag, to be comforted, to be told I was heroic, even that I was a damn fool. It all had to be contained inside; I had to act as if nothing earthshaking was facing me. Even Rep, the only one I could talk to, had little contact with me.

During this time a close friend was in the hospital for an appendectomy. I can still remember the self-discipline it took not to blurt out my plans when I went to see her. I was like a balloon blown up to the bursting point that could not find some release from the internal pressure. Taking my physical exam was the only task I had to complete. The doctor, who was either a party member or very sympathetic, had a small office. I stripped and he gave me a thorough going-over. Other than that, and getting my passport and visa for France, there wasn't anything I could do. So I waited.

It was a lonely, painful time, possible to bear only because I was proud of my decision and felt a commitment to something bigger than myself. I lied and told my family and my friends that at the end of June or in the first part of July I'd be going to work for the national office of the American Student Union in New York. Dad was outraged that I was not planning to continue my schooling, that I would work for something he thought of as a leftist, radical, subversive, socialist, communistic organization. I was a disgrace to the family, a disappointment as a son.

Most of all he was mad because I was disrespectful of him and his values and because I was not planning to carry on the Rubin name as he had envisioned. Finally we came to a sort of standoff. I asked only that I be able to live at home until I left in a couple of months; then I would be completely self-supporting. I was adamant that he could not dictate how I was to run my life. I stayed in our house as little as possible and when there kept to my room, because the situation was so tense. There I smoked my pipe and pounded away on my old typewriter, writing poems, trying to finish my novel. This was the way I kept my calm, contained the mixture of my emotions. I could write poems and fiction that told of my anger at a society that was malfunctioning, writings that expressed my disdain for those who couldn't or wouldn't see what was wrong.

I was sad because my mother, to whom I was deeply attached, was so unhappy, both about my leaving and about my alienation from the family. My feelings about her were so mixed, always in conflict. My sister, Audrey, had gone to college when I was seven, then married and moved away by the time I was ten; so Mom had turned her attention in my direction. I loved her and wanted to please and protect her, but, at the same time, I was angry because she didn't stand up to my father, either for me or for herself. We had been very close in my earlier years and yet, in my later teens, a wall of misunderstanding had grown between us. She was a housewife very typical of that earlier era, subordinate in almost everything to her husband. Her status, and the success in the world that mattered to her, was predicated on the cleanliness of her house, the excellence of her cooking, and the upbringing of her children. In my anger at her I was not able to understand that, as she saw it, she had no choice. Divorce was unthinkable, not a conceivable alternative. My strong feelings about the need for the equality of women stem in large part from my antipathy to my parents' relationship. During those months I barely exchanged any words with my father. I refused to listen to what he said; what I tried to explain, he would not understand. The scenario never changed. We were at a complete impasse.

CHAPTER 2

Los Angeles to Le Havre

Somehow the time passed, a time in which I often felt suspended, out of touch with the world around me. I tired of either not telling my friends the truth, or lying when I couldn't skirt a direct question. At the end of June the welcome call came from Rep, who told me to report to an office in downtown Los Angeles at 9:30 in the morning on July 2 with a single, small bag of clothes and toiletries, ready to go. On the night of the first, I announced my departure to my folks. Mom was worried and tearful, Dad stony-faced, not saying a word.

The next morning I kissed my mother good-bye, said so long to my father, and walked the two short blocks to 3rd & La Brea to catch the streetcar. Downtown I got off at Spring and walked down the street for several blocks. At the appointed time, I entered an old, run-down office building with a rickety elevator and went to room 303. Unoccupied by any tenant, it had apparently been borrowed for this meeting. In it were a small, ancient, battered flattop desk and a few wooden folding chairs; there was no phone and no files, or anything on the walls. The single window was smeared with accumulated dirt. A tall, thin man with a double chin who identified himself only as Jim introduced me to four other men who were also volunteering. He gave each of us a few dollars for food on the trip to New York and a Greyhound bus ticket, the cheapest mode of cross-country transportation. He checked our passports one by one, each of which was stamped "NOT VALID FOR TRAVEL TO SPAIN," as were all passports issued after March 4, 1937.

"Are any of you carrying any weapons, you know, pistols, revolvers, anything? Do you have any books or pamphlets of a political nature, whether about Spain or not? I'm checking on these things, for there should be nothing on you or in your possession to give evidence as to your destination."

Although each of us answered with a negative, he inspected our luggage anyway. Then he told us the address of a small hotel in Manhattan, our New York destination, where our rent would be paid by "the Committee." There was no mention of who was organizing our trip, although I assumed that it was the Communist party. I later found out that the party was the organizer and recruiter of personnel and that the Spanish Republic was the supplier of funds for our transportation. Fred appeared to be going down a checklist. There was no mention of pay, insurance, or any benefits in the event we were wounded or killed. There was no contract or agreement offered or signed as to the duration of our stay. The talk was only of how we would get to New York and how we were to act en route—nothing of the trip beyond.

At about that time, Martha Gellhorn, the well-known author and journalist, wrote the following in *Colliers* magazine about the volunteers: "There are no Congressional medals, no Distinguished Service Crosses, no bonuses for soldiers' families, no newspaper glory. And what you get paid every day would buy a soft drink and a pack of cigarettes in America, but no more. Six pesetas which is about sixty cents."

Because the rest of the group had come from places other than Los Angeles, I was the only person known to the organizing committee, so Jim appointed me group leader and gave me the telephone number to contact in New York and the procedure to be followed. He told me whom and how to call for instructions for our next move. After a very short meeting we left for the bus depot, which was within walking distance. We spread out in single file, ten or fifteen yards apart, as per his instructions, so as not to look like a group. Jim kept parallel with us on the sidewalk across the street.

There were no parades, no bands playing inspiring marches, no banners unfurled. Since we had been sworn to secrecy, there were no friends or lovers to cheer us on. Even this anonymous man who had briefed us stood in the background, unacknowledged by us, checking that all went as planned. We were to play the role of ordinary men who were going by the cheapest means possible to New York; we weren't even to act as if we knew each other en route, except as casual seatmates. I knew my companions only by first name. Their histories I learned, in a limited way, only when we were in Paris.

What an odd bunch we were!

Mark, a professional card player from San Francisco, was the oldest of the group, a couple of years past thirty. Before joining he had been a dealer in a poker club. Slim and wiry, he had a dark, heavy beard that always seemed to call for shaving. He was almost taciturn, never given to small talk. I never understood why he had decided to come on this journey. In none of our subsequent but limited conversations did he volunteer any explanation, here, along the way, or later in Spain. He avoided answering questions about his background with great skill. He never evidenced any real political or social interest. In Spain he did his job, never shirking but never volunteering. He was neither friendly nor unfriendly—the consummate loner.

Hera, who had worked at the Kaiser Steel plant in southern California, was born in Armenia. He was the second oldest, about twenty-eight. Short, very stocky, but powerfully built, he seemed to communicate mainly in grunts. He did not appear to be comfortable in English, although on occasion, when angry, he demonstrated a good command of the language. He was a party member, deeply committed, drawing his strength, it seemed, from the atrocities that had been visited upon him and his family in the Old Country. He was serious, conscientious, and friendly. Once we got to Spain he was always helpful.

Al, an unemployed construction worker, was a presence when needed, never late for an assignment, cheerful, and even-tempered. Almost nondescript in appearance, he was the kind of person who is not easily noticed in a crowd. About twenty-five, he had headed an Unemployed Council in San Diego. His slight frame belied a great strength. In Spain, at the front, he was known as one of the dependables.

John was a handsome, blond-haired nineteen-year-old who had lied about his age and was traveling with a borrowed passport that showed him to be twenty-one. He never told us his real name. To him, the whole idea of Spain was just a wonderful adventure. His face already showed a sagging hint of dissipation, even though he was still in his teens. He was talkative, ever-smiling, quick to take a drink when it was available, nonpolitical, and more interested in women than anything else. He had a sixth sense that told him where and when alcohol was available, and a radar for locating willing women combined with the good looks and manners to attract them. I wondered who had recruited him.

Our Greyhound bus pulled out of the station on time for the long, hot, boring trip of four days and nights across the country without air conditioning. We had to change buses several times along the way. The five of us seated ourselves around the bus from front to back, not sitting together. We had no opportunity to shower, and some of us began to stink, particularly Hera, who evidently didn't believe in deodorants. More and more, no one wanted to sit next to him. My comrades began to whisper complaints to me, their "leader," about him, as if I could do something. I tried to sit next to him, but it got a bit much even for me.

We crossed the Mojave Desert, then traveled through Arizona, New Mexico, through the Texas Panhandle, into Arkansas and onto the central plains, and then across the Mississippi River and through the eastern states. Unfortunately, we passed through much of the fascinating scenery of Western America at night. Our daytime view was mostly of desert or flat farmland. After the first few cattle herds, they all seemed to look alike. What a distorted view of America that trip gave me. One state blended into another, and each rolled by without much meaning or distinction. When we stopped in a city, the bus depot was usually in the ratty part of town, and we got no sense of what that city was really like.

We were not supposed to communicate openly with each other, and so there was little chance to develop any real sense of group solidarity. At the stops, we stretched, walked back and forth to get the kinks out, and snacked at the bus station lunch counters on hamburgers, bowls of soup or chili, and coffee or Cokes. When we shaved, it was in the lavatory washbasins. On the bus we read, dozed, looked at the scenery, and talked occasionally with our seatmates, who kept changing as passengers got on and off—anything to help pass the boring miles.

John started flirting with a young woman on the bus who had boarded at Yuma, Arizona. They quickly became a twosome, kissing and fondling each other when it was dark. On the third day, at one of the stops, he maneuvered so that he and I were alone in the lavatory. We were standing next to each other, using the urinals. After looking under the toilet doors to make sure that none of the stalls were occupied, he whispered to me, "I'm going to get off with Martha at the next decent-sized city at which the bus stops and spend a night or two with her. Then I'll catch a bus and meet you guys at the hotel in New York." I had no real authority, yet I had been appointed group leader. I was aghast. What was I to do? Ours was a muted but heated conversation, as we stood at the urinals, constantly glancing over our shoulders to make sure no one came in and could overhear us.

"For Christsake, John, you can't do this! We might be gone by the time you get there. I don't know how many days there are before we have to board our ship."

"Why not? She's good looking and willing and I want to. It's not going to harm anyone. And who knows when I'll have another chance to have a woman when we get there."

"Look, I understand, I'm just as horny as you, I'd like to, too, but it's too risky. I'm not allowed to give you the phone number that Jim gave me, so that if we leave you'll have nowhere to go, no one to contact. What's more, even if you do arrive before we leave, if they know what you've done they probably won't let you come. If you don't arrive with the group they'll call you unfit, irresponsible, and who knows what other names. But outside of calling you names, they'll say that you're not the type that can be depended upon in battle. You know they'll scratch you off the list of those who are going."

Our discussion continued, but my arguments seemed to make no dent. I was beginning to make my own judgment that maybe it was better if he didn't go to Spain. Finally, an idea came to me that worked.

"Since she is also going to New York, how about if you come through with us as planned but make a date to spend a night or two with her when we get there? When you're with her you can keep in touch with me by phone so that if our departure date is a hurried one you can get back in time."

Grudgingly he agreed. I got back on the bus and collapsed in my seat. So much for my leadership position.

When we finally got off the bus in New York, I disregarded instructions and we walked as a group. I was afraid we would get lost, and I wanted the other men's help in getting to our destination. I rationalized our clustering by thinking that no one in the midst of this horde of strange people on the Manhattan sidewalks would know who we were. So I clutched the little map Jim had given me in Los Angeles, and off we went, constantly checking street signs. When we got to the hotel on the west side of Manhattan and were assigned rooms, John quickly shaved and showered and, with our reluctant and envious blessings, went off by subway to keep his date with Martha, his girlfriend from the bus. He didn't appear until the second day, but he did keep in touch with me by phone.

The next morning, following security instructions, I went to a pay phone on the street, several blocks from the hotel to prevent any possible wiretapping, and nervously called the contact number. A male voice answered with a noncommittal "Yes."

"This is Hank Rubin from Los . . ." I started to say more, but the male voice at the other end immediately cut me off in midsentence.

"Wednesday morning promptly at 10:30 be at the Young Travel Agency at 8th Avenue and 38th Street. It's actually on 38th. Talk only to Frank. He'll give you your tickets. Go by yourself, alone, but take with you all the passports of your group. He'll check them, give you everything you need, and tell you where to go and when to be there. Have you got it?"

"Wednesday, 10:30. Frank, at Young Travel on 38th near 8th."

The line clicked and went silent. His curt manner and the way he cut me off reimpressed upon me that security was a key issue. Actually I felt good that I was part of something so important. It was like a scenario from a spy movie. At the appointed time I walked to 38th Street to see Frank as instructed. Seated next to his desk, which was only partially partitioned off from the rest of the office, was a young man in his midtwenties who greeted me with a smile but said nothing. Frank took the five passports. With hardly a word he checked each one carefully, inserted the ship tickets and boarding passes between the pages of each one, and gave them to me one by one. Then he gave instructions.

"Go to Pier 70 at 9:00 A.M. the day after tomorrow. That's Friday. Have your squad take the bus that stops at the corner of your hotel. Remember not to act as a unit. That is the most critical thing. Most important is not to let anyone know who you are or where you are going. Impress that on each member of your group."

He made me repeat my instructions three times, until he was convinced I really knew what to do, and then he introduced me to the young man waiting there with him.

"This is Fred, who will be on the ship with you. If you have any problems in your group get in touch with him, but only if there is a real problem. If there are any changes in plans, he'll contact you on board. Just before disembarking, he'll tell you what to do and where to go when you get to France. The command that you have been operating under, not to be an obvious group, that none of you know your destination, is still in force. This discipline is to be continued on board. If anything, it now becomes more important."

I gave Frank a group of five letters that I had written to my family while in Los Angeles, letters that I had postdated. Fred was to mail one each week in the order I had dated them. In them I said that I was doing well in my new job and told a little about life in New York, things that I had made up. Fred and I quietly shook hands and smiled at each other, but he said nothing, and responding to his silence, neither did I. Finally, Frank stood, came around the desk, and put his hand on my shoulder. Then he, too, shook my hand warmly and softly said, "Good luck and do a good job when you get there."

Our brief stay in New York, only a couple of days, was uneventful. Strangely, I can remember very little else about being in the big city for the first time. It seems amazing to me that I cannot, as it must have been so different from anything that I had ever experienced. Surely my writer's antennae must have been quivering. I do remember eating in a Horn and Hardart Automat and being fascinated by being able to choose what I wanted by putting coins into a slot. I then took out the dish of food I'd wanted, already prepared, from behind a little glass door.

One of the instructions from Jim in Los Angeles had been that we were not to carry anything that might give us away. That was quite different from the message given the first volunteer groups, who had been instructed to scour the city's army and navy stores to buy uniforms, ammunition belts, and so forth. As the French government began to crack down on the passage of volunteers, our organizers changed the pattern of handling the men, striving to make us inconspicuous.

On Friday morning we checked out of the hotel without having to pay for our rooms. We got on a city bus and rode to Pier 70, still pretending not to know each other. There loomed the *Queen Elizabeth,* huge and exciting. In the midst of a lot of noise, cars and taxis discharging passengers, people saying their good-byes, luggage carts, workers and travelers and equipment of all kinds, we separately presented our tickets to the ship's agents, who also checked our passports and visas. One by one we walked up the gangplank carrying our small bags. As we reached the deck of the ship we were again checked off a list by the steward, who then turned us over to porters who carried our bags and showed us where our tiny third-class staterooms were.

"If you'll give me your baggage tickets, sir, I'll get the rest of your luggage and bring it to your room."

"This is the only piece of luggage I have."

He looked at me disbelievingly. It was a dead giveaway that we were not just tourists. We should have had at least a couple of bags. We did not have cabins to ourselves. Each small third-class compartment had two bunks. My newly assigned roommate luckily turned out to be a volunteer, as well, although not one of our Los Angeles five. It took only a few sentences between Sigmund and me before we suspected each other's destination. Then it took very little verbal maneuvering to confirm our suspicions. After gulps and with crossed fingers we broke the commandment of silence, fortunately with no repercussions. We knew that we were comrades. He was from Brooklyn, where he had been teaching Hebrew and Yiddish. About twenty-five, tall, and slim, he had a wiry build that did not suggest a powerful person, although he was very strong. His narrow, slightly craggy face was decorated with a full mustache that I envied. In order to look more mature, I had once tried to grow one but had achieved only a dirty upper lip.

Sig and I hit it off very well. Both of us were interested in music, art, and books. Our politics were the same, and although he was much better read than I he didn't lord it over me. He was as easygoing as I, so we didn't have clashes of temperament. At night we exchanged confidences and shared our dreams. I was even able to say a little about my fears of combat. Every so often the possibility of death or disfigurement would bring my fear into consciousness. With him I could let it come out without feeling that I was weak or unmanly. Stowing our meager belongings took but a few minutes, and we didn't even have much of an argument about who would have the upper berth. We tossed a coin and I lost, but, what the hell, I could sleep anywhere!

Everything was so exciting. We raced up to the deck where we watched passengers arriving at the last minute who rushed on board, porters carrying luggage, and the ship's crew performing their departure functions. Finally, the gangplanks were pulled back. With much hooting of horns, tugs slowly separated the ship from the dock and pushed us out into the channel to begin our journey out to sea. When we passed the Statue of Liberty, which my father had seen as a young boy emigrating from Russia more than fifty years earlier, I wondered whether I would survive to see it again.

Sigmund told me that he had heard that the contingent of volunteers on board had now swollen from our original five from Los Angeles to more than thirty from various parts of the country and Canada. It was not difficult to pick out many of them, because they didn't fit the profile of ordinary folk going to Europe. Many of our volunteers were of the working class, wearing new, very inexpensive, and ill-fitting clothes. Those were days when "going to Europe" was reserved mainly for the rich; few others could think of it, even traveling third-class. This was the time before airplane travel, and that meant that at least a week was necessary just to get to Europe. We were a group of unsophisticated young men who certainly didn't look like affluent vacationers or people going abroad on business.

I had no idea what sort of organization there was among the volunteers on board. The man to whom Sig reported was someone we didn't discuss. Besides Sig, I knew for certain only the four from the L.A. group who reported to me and the man to whom I was to report, if necessary. I saw Fred regularly at mealtimes for, by chance, he had been assigned to the table next to mine. But we didn't talk until just before we landed in France.

My way of trying to look like an individual who was not part of any group was to tell everyone that I spoke to in our third-class area that I was going to wander around Europe doing stories for the UCLA *Daily Bruin.* The story of my having a newspaper assignment abroad seemed quite reasonable, at least to me. I don't know if anyone believed my story, or if they knew I was going to Spain, but after the first day or so some of the passengers acted as if they knew my secret. Sometimes they would smile when I told my cock-and-bull stories, or wink to signify that they knew what it was all about, or talk about the war and show their sympathies for the Loyalists.

I suspect that one or more of the volunteers hadn't been able to hold his tongue, had told someone "in confidence." I understood the need to talk because it was hard for me to keep from shouting out what we were going to do. Now that we were out of the country, actually on our way, I was even more excited. The horror of battle was far away. Certainly for virtually all of us, except possibly for some seamen volunteers, this was the first time out of the country. I had never before even crossed the border into Mexico, which was only a little more than a hundred miles south of Los Angeles. This was certainly my first time ever on a big passenger ship. Sig and I roamed the ship together. On the second day we were tempted and slipped under the velvet cord that blocked access up the stairs toward first class. First we wandered among the cabins and marveled at their spaciousness, peeking through the open doors of cabins that were being cleaned.

Up on the next level, in the salons, the walnut paneling was polished to a high burnish and the furniture was lush and really comfortable. The passengers were far more expensively dressed. Even their casual clothes seemed far better than the best we'd seen in third class.

At first, our reaction was one of amazement at the elegance we saw, the level of comfort that was available in first class.

"Hey, how fancy, what class!"

"It sure would be more comfortable not being so crowded. And I'll bet that the food is not only fancier but also a lot better than what we're served."

But as we were commenting about this to each other, a note of anger crept into our discussion, and we became furious that such class distinctions should exist.

Not many minutes after we'd started to roam the first-class part of the ship, a purser saw us. Politely, but firmly, he reprimanded us. "I'm afraid you gentlemen will have to go down to your own area. You are not allowed up here."

That ocean voyage was a fantastic experience. Until then I had never really comprehended how big the ocean is. As we kept sailing day after day without sighting land, I was overwhelmed by its vastness. It seemed as if it would never end. I was familiar with the Pacific Ocean, of course, but this was a wholly different experience than standing on the shoreline looking out at the horizon. Once in a while, when the weather was clear, from Los Angeles we could see Catalina Island off in the distance. But that seemed only to put a cap on the Pacific's vastness. The Atlantic's immensity, once I found myself in the middle of it, was hard for me to assimilate. It seemed to go on forever.

We landed first at Southampton, England, where a good portion of the passengers disembarked. We, along with about half of the travelers, those going on to France, were not allowed to get off the boat because our stay there was only a few hours. From our deck we looked down at the dock, at the men working with trucks and dollies, at the lines that secured the ship. I wondered whether I would ever set foot in England, the land of tall, slim men in dark suits, bowlers, and furled umbrellas, the land of Shakespeare and Chaucer. Would I live to do so? And, more important, if I did survive, would I ever have enough money to afford such a trip?

It took only a few hours more of sailing south across the English Channel before we docked, disembarked at Le Havre, and went through immigration and customs. The thirty of us seemed to me to be a very visible group, standing out from the regular passengers even though we intermingled with them. My answer to "What is the purpose of your visit?" was "Pleasure and work as a journalist." With my fingers in my pants pocket tightly crossed, I watched the grim, impassive face of the official as he hesitated. He looked at my passport photo and then at me several times. Finally he stamped my passport, and I could relax. Neither the immigration officials nor national police singled out any of the volunteers for special attention.

Sig had told me of a previous group from New York, who, before disembarkation at this same dock, had been herded into the ship's main salon. Because they had bought uniforms, ammunition belts, boots, and other equipment before leaving New York, they were clearly warriors-to-be. In the salon, a U.S. consular officer, flanked by a half-dozen gendarmes, made a short speech saying that he knew where they were trying to go. Not only were they not going to get there, but to do so was against the law. The U.S. government, he said, would pay the passage of anyone who wanted to go back home, even if they wanted to take a short vacation in Paris first. But no one from that contingent took him up on the offer or responded to the threat. Then the French Immigration Office, apparently under pressure from the United States, announced that everyone in third class would have to show evidence of being self-supporting while in France. As none of that group had much money, they pooled everything they had, which came to $96. The first in line showed the bills and then passed the roll back to the comrade in back of him. Each was accepted as financially self-sufficient with $96. The immigration personnel must have known what was happening, but they went along with the farce, perhaps because they resented the pressure put upon them by a foreign government, perhaps because of their personal politics.

After passing through Immigration and Customs, we gathered outside. The first thing many of us did was to buy newspapers at the kiosk outside the building, so that we could find out what was happening in the war. The daily ship's bulletins had given little or no news from Spain. Getting a signal from Fred, we crossed the road to the train station. There we were met by a couple of representatives of the underground railroad that would eventually move us to the border and across into Spain. They gave us tickets and directed us to board the boat-train to Paris, which we did without incident.

Hank Rubin, as a child, with his father, Benjamin W. Rubin,
and sister Audrey.

Fannye Rubin (Rubin's mother), *second from right*,
with her family, the Seeligs.

Courtyard of the base hospital, Valls, Spain, 1937.

Granville Walker Paine, age 22, 1937,
one of Rubin's comrades who was killed in Spain.

MINISTERIO DE DEFENSA NACIONAL

Comisión Española para la Retirada
de Combatientes Extranjeros

RUBIN HENRI .... *combatiente*

de nacionalidad Americana .... *forma parte del*

convoy que ha de pasar la frontera francesa, el día

de ....

Barcelona, 27 *de* Noviembre .... *de 193* 8 ......

EL GENERAL PRESIDENTE,

Ministerio de Defensa Nacional's authorization of Hank Rubin's
departure from Spain, November 27, 1938.

Hank Rubin, 1939, newly returned from Spain.
Photo by Don Ornitz.

Hank Rubin during World War II, Brisbane, Australia, 1944.

Hank Rubin, 1996. Photo by Lillian Rubin.

CHAPTER
3

Le Havre to Carcassonne

The boat train, with thirty excited young men, pulled out of Le Havre promptly at five in the evening. It was headed for Paris, where we arrived early the next morning. During the first hours of our trip it was still daylight, and I was introduced to a whole new world. The architecture of the ancient farmhouses and other buildings we passed was strange and exciting, as was the beautiful, lush green Normandy landscape with its cows and apple orchards that dotted the land.

"Hey Sig, look at that farm!"

"So what's so different about it?"

"It's so clean. I don't mean clean, it's more like someone came and raked everything into place, picked up every leaf, dug up every weed. It's like the whole thing was manicured."

Everything was so different from what I knew at home, the shape of the railway cars, even the sound of the train's whistle. I'm afraid that I made a pest of myself during the first part of the trip with "Look at that" every few minutes, so that Sig must have welcomed darkness, which shut me down. When the train slowed and slid to a stop in Paris, I gawked at the tall, arching glass roof of the station, which was so enchanting and again so unlike any train terminal that I had ever seen.

My orders were to collect the men of my group on the station platform in Paris and watch for a signal from Fred. We stood together, waiting nervously. Soon he passed by me and cautiously pointed toward one of the men standing in the station where arriving passengers were met. I looked and saw a tall, slim Frenchman with a burly black mustache. He was wearing a black suit and had a small black beret on top of his head. I caught his eye and nodded to him, and then without a word or gesture of acknowledgement he turned and started walking out of the building, through the crowd toward the parking lot. We followed, keeping back just a little, anxious to keep up and yet not so closely as to seem to be attached to him. We were becoming good at being unobtrusive. Outside, still not talking, he put us into his small bus. Then he went back into the station while we waited for a short time until he brought another small group to join us.

Battling the early-morning traffic of Parisians going to work, he drove through a maze of crowded streets. All the while, I was excitedly taking in this new city that was passing by the bus windows. We finally arrived at one of the city's outer districts, which was known as the "red belt of Paris." This area got its name from the fact that the communities that composed it were almost completely working-class, and most had communist or socialist mayors and councils. Our chauffeur, who spoke no English and during our trip said virtually nothing in any language, drove us into a street of an undistinguished, working-class district lined with uniformly drab buildings. He left us off in front of a dingy hotel and pointed us inside. There the clerk directed our Los Angeles contingent to a room with five cots on the second floor.

We were together and alone and able to talk for the first time since leaving that drab office back home. After stowing our gear, we sat on the cots, smoking and recounting our impressions of our long trip. We introduced ourselves and then began to speculate about the next leg of our journey. After about twenty minutes or so, the desk clerk knocked on the door and indicated that we were to come downstairs. From the lobby we followed him down the block to a small movie theater. There we joined the rest of the men from the ship. Because the theater was open to the public only in the evening, it would serve as our daytime meeting-place. Our appearance in this neighborhood could hardly have escaped notice by the area's residents, but the neighborhood apparently was so solidly "left" that the organizers felt fairly secure.

When Pierre, the man who had taken charge of us, informed us that we might be there as long as a week or more, I felt let down. My excitement dribbled out as he talked. I wanted to cry, to protest, to stamp my feet, to demand instant transport to Spain.

Pierre also warned us: "Some previous volunteers, perhaps assuming everyone in this district is pro-Spain, boasted to people they met in cafes or on the streets about where they were going, and some of those who talked were arrested. Since you are going to be part of an army, you must consider this a command of silence and be as unobtrusive as possible. You are under army discipline from this moment on. No getting drunk! No getting into fights! No getting arrested! Again, this is an order."

He would have been much more successful in getting our cheerful cooperation if he hadn't been so prissy in his manner. His attitude seemed off-base, as if he were talking to youngsters—so much so that I had a child's reaction. I wanted to disobey him, just to thwart him.

When he stopped instructing us on our behavior, he became fascinating. He told us in considerable detail about the real problems to be faced in getting us across the border. Both the French border police and the very active patrols that had been established by the embargo of the Non-Intervention Pact were on the lookout for Brigade volunteers.

"Also, there are fascist bastards here in Paris, as well as in the south, who are trying to seek us out. Sometimes they may be paid agents, sometimes just ideologues or gangsters of the right wing. While our volunteers from central and eastern Europe and the Balkan countries are special targets, all of you are strongly cautioned, actually ordered, not to attract attention, not to tell anyone who you are, where you are going, no matter how sympathetic the listener might appear."

To our cries of impatience he could only counsel us not to be in such a hurry: "Patience, patience, we're doing everything we can. We can't just put you on a train and ship you to the border and have you walk across. We have to get you close to the line without attracting attention, then move you up into the foothills of the Pyrenees, have guides ready to take you across, and make sure that you can slip by the guards. We have to feed you, house and hide you along the way, and have someone to meet you on the other side. The passage is surest for you if at least one of the pair of guards is sympathetic, and we know some who are. To do this we have to have the assistance of a lot of comrades along the line and, most of all, your help and cooperation."

When he began to explain what the problems were, I simmered down and didn't focus so much on his mannerisms. If only he had started out that way, instead of lecturing us. But Pierre was very knowledgeable about international affairs, and he explained to us about the Non-Intervention Pact and what it meant to us.

He told us that the socialist premier of France, Léon Blum, favored the Republic and wanted to help. But Blum was afraid that France was vulnerable to armed aggression from Hitler on its eastern border and Mussolini in the southeast. Both nations had been threatening France. What with their invasions of the Rhineland, Austria, Abyssinia, and Ethiopia, and with their threatening gestures in the direction of France, they couldn't be trusted not to act. Blum had been in office only a little more than a month before the start of the Franco rebellion. While an overwhelming popular majority in France supported the Republic, he was faced with deep divisions within his government and therefore he felt that his hold on his office was shaky. Unlike the United States, where the president is elected for four years, in France the premier can be voted out of office by a vote of the parliament at any time. French president Albert Lebrun had told Blum at the start of the revolt that giving arms to Spain would probably lead either to a war of invasion or to a revolution within France, started by the right wing and much of the army.

Pierre explained that when Blum had turned to England for support, he found that the very reactionary government of that country was solidly opposed to the Spanish Republic and adamant in its support of Franco. Without British backup, Blum couldn't stand up to the threats from the Axis, so he argued for an international Non-Intervention Pact to be monitored by the League of Nations. His belief was that if outside help to both sides were stopped, the Republic could crush the opposition. The weakness of his thinking was twofold: First, the League had neither the desire nor the capacity to take any forceful actions, as had been demonstrated by its lack of initiative in such places as Manchuria, the Rhineland, Ethiopia, Austria, and Albania. Second, it was wishful thinking on Blum's part to believe that the Axis powers would honor their signatures.

Blum's proposal for nonintervention was made within a couple of weeks of the beginning of the rebellion, but the League took until early September just to get its twenty-six nations to meet in London. Then there were interminable squabbles and delays until the pact was actually adopted. The prohibition against men going (or being sent) to Spain hadn't even been a part of the original pact; that prohibition wasn't put into effect until the following February (that is, in 1938). By the time of the first signing, huge shipments of armaments and other war matériel and thousands upon thousands of soldiers had been sent from Germany and Italy to support Franco. Even more important, all the troops of the Spanish Army of Africa had been ferried over to the mainland. These fighting units from Morocco, which had been under Franco's command before the revolt, were considered the best fighting force in the Spanish army, and they formed much of his striking power.

Predictably, the pact was immediately ignored by Italy and Germany, while Britain put tremendous pressure on France to honor its provisions. During the first month of the war, that is, until August 1, the French government and private arms dealers sold and shipped small amounts of Swiss, Czech, and Belgian arms to the Republic. In the short period of a few weeks, the Republic was able to buy a few planes for which French author André Malraux recruited international pilots to fly across the border into combat.

But on August 2, fearful of splitting his United Front government at home or of alienating Britain, which was putting such pressure on him, Blum closed the borders. Britain had already unilaterally barred sales of arms in July. The result was that, contrary to international law, the elected government of Spain could not buy the means to defend itself. During this period, the United States, while preaching noninvolvement, permitted the Texaco Company to ship large quantities of oil to the insurgents, claiming that it was not war matériel. Ford, General Motors, and Studebaker shipped twelve thousand vehicles to Germany, most of which were immediately transshipped to Franco. The Soviet Union was signatory to the pact as well, but after the demonstration of gross violation by the Axis powers, the USSR openly declared itself not bound by the agreement and began to send aid to Madrid.

Before the border was closed, a large number of Frenchman had quietly slipped across the border to help the Republic. They did this without any connection with an organized movement. Now Frenchmen, as well as internationals like us, had to be sent along the underground route.

When Pierre had finished his explanation, I felt relieved that the organizers of our travel knew what we were up against and were probably handling the situation with skill. They would probably get me there in one piece, and I wouldn't land in jail. While I didn't like it and was still impatient, I felt that I could live with the delay without coming apart.

Paris was the center for the mobilization and movement of the volunteers. The housing and forwarding of the men going to Spain was supported by the Maison des Syndicates (union center) and some other worker organizations. The Communist party, under the direction of the Third International (Comintern) representative Togliatti, was active not only in generating that support but also in directing its application, getting us housing and moving us south across the border. Although it was the central mover, the Communist party kept its role in the background as much as possible.

Each morning at breakfast, we waited for notification that we would be moved south that day. If not, we were free to roam the city. On the second morning we were told that nothing would happen that day, so right after breakfast Sigmund and I got onto the subway and went to the center of the city. It was July 14, Bastille Day, which had been observed with a parade as part of its celebration for more than a century. The observance of this holiday, the day of French Independence, was much more intense, much more widespread than our observance of July Fourth in the United States. I remember that, as a kid back in Portland, about the only thing my friends and I would do is shoot off a few small firecrackers on the Fourth. The radio might carry the broadcast of a parade somewhere in the nation, and there might be a picture of a flag or some parade marchers on the front page of the *Oregonian*. Once when I was visiting my aunt and uncle in Eau Claire, Wisconsin, there was a barbecue in the town and some fireworks.

On that French Independence Day, Sigmund and I got off at the metro station closest to the Place de la Concorde, where Marie Antoinette had been guillotined some 150 years earlier. The day was warm and bright and sunny but not too hot. As I looked up at the sky, the background of white, puffy, broken clouds in a blue sky seemed only to emphasize the beauty of the city and its buildings, with its turrets, gargoyles, and dark grey slate roofs that seemed so different to me, so exotic.

Because of the depression in France and the rising militancy of the union movement, the parade had become much more of a political affair than it had been earlier. The United Front against Fascism (better known simply as the United Front or the Popular Front) had moved into organizing a major portion of the parade. This year the front was focusing on two main themes. The first was to protest the right-wing drift of the government, which they saw as a threat to the working class and particularly the union movement; the second was to give support to the Republic of Spain while at the same time crying defiance to all fascists, whether in Germany or Italy or at home.

Even though a very large portion of the parade had been organized by the political left, those who marched came from the widest variety of political viewpoints: from the ultra left to the very conservative. Many participants represented apolitical cultural associations. They came every year, regardless of any political theme being put forward, to celebrate the end of the monarchy, the fall of the hated Bastille, and the establishment of the Republic. Men, women, and children from trade unions, neighborhood groups, political organizations, drama ensembles, regional representatives from Alsace, Brittany, Normandy, and other provinces that I had never heard of came to participate. This year there were so many groups and marchers that they had to be assembled in fifty-two adjoining streets, from which they marched, unit by unit, to meld into the main parade.

The actual parade route was down the Avenue des Champs Élysées, a wide boulevard in the center of the city that is lined with chestnut trees and broad sidewalks. The mile-long avenue starts at the Arc de Triomphe and gently slopes down to the Place de la Concorde. When we arrived it was lined with spectators, at places fifteen or twenty deep. The tables of the many cafes that fronted the avenue seemed to cover almost the entire broad sidewalk, and every seat was filled. Coming down the avenue itself was an uninterrupted line of parading units, a stream that lasted for hours.

To make sure that the parade and demonstration remained under control, uniformed officers were everywhere, recruited from both the police forces of Paris and those of the national government. It appeared to me that there were thousands of them, many on active duty along the Champs Élysées and more as a large reserve waiting in police buses parked on side streets.

The celebration was festive and at the same time very political: Children in baby buggies, union banners, placards, balloons, working clothes, fancy dress, regional outfits, mime troupes, clowns, costumes from the French Revolution, marching bands of all kinds. Except for a small, silent contingent of restaurant workers who were making some kind of protest, they were a noisy lot.

There was a bubbling of excitement among the marchers as they talked or sang. They laughed, locked arms, waved to friends along the route, occasionally even did some dance steps; a feeling of warmth and comradeship exuded from their ranks. When their attention was caught by an occasional small group along the way who shouted hostile comments at them, they stiffened and directed stony glares, raised their banners a bit higher, shouted slogans. A few, particularly the younger men, had to be restrained from rushing off to the sidewalk to attack their hecklers. A heavy concentration of gendarmes surrounded the few small groups of counter-demonstrators, both protecting and containing them. All sorts of banners and slogans on buildings and trees along the route shouted support of the

Spanish Republic: *Vive Espagne,* or *Bas à Franco.* Placards on the street gave the slogan advanced by *L'Humanité* (the communist newspaper): "With Spain for the Safety of France."

Sig and I started at the bottom of the avenue at the parade's end, the Place de la Concorde. The noise and color of a hundred flapping flags that hung alongside the Tuileries seemed a part of the celebration. From the bottom of the avenue, we slowly walked in the street, against the flow, observing all the marchers and banners, savoring the action. Every so often we noticed a comrade or two from our group of volunteers who was marching in the parade, but only a few together, blending in with one group or another, not violating the orders to keep our identity secret.

Feeling the nervous energy of the crowd, experiencing the support for our cause, it would have been impossible for us to stay out of this demonstration. So when we got up to the top of the street, we slipped into the contingent of the plumbers' union, which, as we arrived, was just starting around the circle of the Arc de Triomphe, positioning itself for its march down the avenue. We marched with them back down toward the Place de la Concord, where we had started and where the units disbanded. The camaraderie we felt as we joined their ranks reinforced our belief that we were on the right path, a part of a great and just worldwide movement, that we belonged to something fine and decent.

To return to our shabby quarters after the parade and excitement seemed anticlimactic, so Sigmund and I went roaming around the city in the early afternoon, both of us exuberant, flying high. We walked through districts with chic stores, fancy homes, and upscale restaurants and into working-class neighborhoods. We gaped at the strange architecture, the signs, the "foreign" cars, particularly the Citroens, which seemed so oddly shaped.

The Brittany crepes that were sold at sidewalk stands—luscious crepes folded into delicious squares stuffed with cheese and ham—served as our inexpensive lunch. For dessert we enjoyed the dessert crepes that were filled with apple slices and sprinkled with sugar. The sidewalk cafes, bustling with action, were lively and enticing. It was strange to us to see men walking arm in arm, unselfconsciously, since at home such a posture would have been derogated as sissy or homosexual.

Just as we turned the corner of a narrow street in a working-class district, a man came out on a little third-floor apartment balcony, raised his arm up in a fascist salute, and repeatedly yelled "Heil Hitler." Patrons of a cafe across the street, where we had stopped, stood up and watched, talking angrily to each other. Within minutes a group of men from neighboring houses and cafes, off work because of the holiday, gathered at the entrance to the apartment building. They yelled up at him, raising their arms with clenched fists. I didn't understand what they were saying, but "Nazi" and "fascist" were a few of the words that needed no translation. They milled in front of the door and cranked themselves up into a mob fever. All of a sudden they broke a pane of the glass door. Someone reached in and opened the door to the apartment building. Then they crowded in and we could see them rush up the stairs.

Once they'd gone inside we couldn't hear anything from where we were standing, nor did we learn what they did to the man who had taunted them, for he had left the balcony and gone inside. The balcony remained empty, the curtained glass doors to it closed, but any act of violence seemed possible, and I could visualize his blood and broken bones.

Opposed to Hitler as I was, this expression of anger out of control, this mob anger, this uncontrolled savagery, frightened me. While on the one hand I too wanted them to kill the bastard, at the same time the intensity of their reaction made me feel guilty and uncomfortable, as if I were participating in that mob. It was different from killing in battle. Then there would be someone shooting back.

After a time, the men who had rushed the stairs began to trickle out in pairs, talking to each other, seeming very angry still. A few came across the street to the cafe where we were sitting, but, unfortunately, we couldn't understand what they were saying or follow their excited conversation.

We walked slowly on, both of us silent for a while, trying to digest what we had experienced. Finally we started talking about it. I turned to Sig.

"I've always had a fear of mobs. I've felt that mobs could always be directed against me. When I was nine we visited at my grandparents' home in Los Angeles. At dinner my great-uncle Jacob Rubin was telling of times in the last century in Borispol, Ukraine, the small city from which my father's family had come. After he'd talked about family, business, and the crops, suddenly the face of this very calm, white-haired old man tightened and tears started to run down his cheeks. Chokingly, he began to tell us of one of the pogroms that he as a child had lived through.

'A Cossack mob came sweeping down the street, shouting "Kill the Jews! Kill the Jews!"—yelling that the Jews had killed Christ and sacrificed Christian babies. Then they forced their way into homes, including our family's, smashing windows. Men and women were hunted out like rats, maimed or killed. These drunken peasants ran into the synagogue across the street and desecrated it, stomping and urinating on the Torah. When our old rabbi came out from his study to protest, they pulled him into the street, formed a circle around him, and then, clapping their hands to set a rhythm, they forced him to dance with a local prostitute. And when he did so they jeered.'

I listened to his story with disbelief that such a thing could happen. Terrified that it could happen to us, to me, I started to cry. My mother came to my chair and put her arms around me, comforting me until my sobbing calmed. I've never forgotten that moment."

We discovered that our reactions were much the same. And it turned out that Sig had had a similar background, that his family had also come from the Ukraine and had had parallel experiences during pogroms.

The two of us wandered on, eventually finding ourselves lost somewhere in the winding streets of the city. We made all sorts of guesses as to which direction to head, but we couldn't even remember for sure the number of the arrondissement in which we were staying. It was a little frightening but also fun. We knew that our hotel was on the right bank of the River Seine, and also that we were still on the right bank, as we hadn't crossed any bridges. But no matter which direction we took, we remained lost. Since we had nothing better to do, we enjoyed our wandering, searching for clues or landmarks that might point us in the right direction.

Suddenly my comrade said, "Don't worry, we'll be all right now. Wait here and I'll get directions."

"What do you mean? Have you seen a map or something?"

"Just stay put."

Sigmund had noticed a man sitting at a small table of a sidewalk cafe reading a Yiddish newspaper. He went up to the man and introduced himself. I watched from the sidewalk. Then Sig sat down and they started to talk. Soon the talk became more agitated and they were shaking their index fingers at each other, apparently very angry. I didn't know what was happening, but I moved over behind Sig. The least I could do, I thought, was to back my comrade. As I listened to them, I finally realized that they were talking in Yiddish, which I didn't understand. I heard their flow of words and understood about every twentieth word, from my limited knowledge of German. All I knew was that they constantly interrupted each other, seeming to challenge each other's every statement. Their argument, I learned afterward, was about who spoke correct Yiddish. Given that Yiddish is a language that takes on the national color of the speaker, it was a foolish argument. But each thought he was right, since they both taught Yiddish and Hebrew, Sigmund in Brooklyn, the Frenchman in Paris. Eventually, both of them having expressed themselves most emphatically, they simmered down to a friendly tone, and we got directions back to our hotel.

When we at last returned to our room, we were still so keyed up that we couldn't let the day end. After the dinner that was provided for us in the small restaurant adjoining our hotel, we decided to go to a movie that both of us had missed in the States, the screen adaptation of Pearl S. Buck's *The Good Earth.* From our French leader we got explicit directions about our route to the theater, both going and coming back. We followed his instructions exactly, but we couldn't find the street signs and started to get that "lost" feeling again.

This time it was I who signaled "don't worry!" I had seen a gendarme standing on a curb. He had an English flag embroidered on the sleeve of his coat, which signified, someone had told me, that he spoke English. We went up to him and I asked politely, "Please, where is the Champs Élysées?" Only instead of saying "chans d'leesay," I pronounced it "CHAMPS DEELEESEEES." When he looked puzzled I repeated the question, enunciating a little more clearly and a little more loudly, exaggerating the words as tourists so often do. After this had gone on a couple of times, he told us to continue on, apparently wanting to get rid of us. We walked several more blocks until we couldn't go any farther because we had come to the River Seine. So back we went the way we had come, until we saw the same gendarme, standing in the same place. I was just about to get into an argument with him when, as we approached, I saw engraved in the concrete of the curbing under his feet the words "Champs Élysées." Feeling like a horse's ass, mad at myself because I was so inept, and angry because it seemed as though all the French were conspiring against me, I turned and followed Pierre's instructions.

We found the movie house, paid our francs, and went inside. But when we got to our seats, the usher kept shining his flashlight on our faces until someone yelled at us in English to tip the usher a franc, which we then did. I sank into my seat, and for quite a while all I could do was collapse into myself, unable to pay much attention to the film.

The next day we had to stay close to the hotel, because we'd been alerted at breakfast that the signal to go south might come at any time. On suggestion from Pierre, we went to a store on the next street to buy berets. The rationale he gave us was that with berets we would look more like tourists. The idea seemed crazy to us, but we did it because it was more like an order than a suggestion. For all of us to wear berets, it seemed to me, would be like wearing a uniform, a badge of identification when we were all together. At the store I didn't know what to buy, as I had never worn any sort of a hat since the beanies I wore as a kid. I finally decided on a medium-sized black beret that I never liked and managed to lose within a few weeks after arriving in Spain.

Late in the afternoon, when the word came that we would leave in a few hours, I checked my group and found one member missing. Once again, it was John. Questioning some of the comrades, I heard that he had boasted to the guys that he was going to a whorehouse near our hotel.

I recruited Hal, a French-speaking comrade from Quebec, to come with me as a translator, and we walked about four blocks, searching out John's destination. In a nondescript two-story building, we walked into a room filled with slightly shopworn red-upholstered furniture. The madam was a slim, gray-haired, beautifully coiffed woman in her fifties. From an ornate radio in the corner came the voice of Josephine Baker. There were six or eight young women, sitting or lying about, who seemed to me to range from eighteen to their mid thirties.

Never before having been to a "house," not speaking the language, I was tense and uncomfortable. I squirmed and blushed, not knowing what to do, how to act. The partially clad young prostitutes sensed my embarrassment and began to tease me, chattering away, making kisses in the air, displaying themselves more provocatively by letting their thin robes fall away. Two of the younger ones got up and came over to me, pressing themselves up against me.

One of them knew some English. "You like us, *cheri?* You very handsome. You want to go upstairs and make fuck? We give you veree good time."

The two of them put their hands over me, caressing me, and laughing at my distress at the same time. But I couldn't respond, could I? My mind said no, but my body didn't listen. I was afraid of venereal disease. And I was the group leader, who had to set an example. How could I square my professed belief in the equality of women with having sex with a prostitute? Wasn't prostitution a social evil that I didn't want to support? Worst of all was my fear. After all, I was a virgin. Would I know what to do? All of these feelings got mixed up with sexual pressures, jumbled hormones, intense curiosity, and desire. The voluptuous, taunting bodies caused me to have a huge and embarrassing erection, and I was scared to death.

I hoarsely whispered, "Hal, go on and ask her about John, if he's here or has been."

He turned to the madam and started to talk. They had an extended conversation in French.

"Well, what did she say ?"

"She said that I talk funny. You know, my Quebec French is not like the way they speak here, and she wanted to know how I learned to speak so well but so different, which province or colony I come from."

"For God's sake, what did she say about John?"

"She was upset that I asked and said that she never talks about her clients."

"Hal, we've got to get some clue about that prick John. He's not disciplined and might have blabbed. I'm going to break the rules. Tell her why we need to know. Even if they are not for Spain, we'll be gone before they can do us any harm. We've got to find him. After all, this is the "red belt." I'm going to take a chance, I'll take the responsibility."

After the two had conversed again in French, she turned to me and said in quite good English, "Oh, why didn't you say so, *monsieur?* Why, every one of us here, all the girls, myself, even the cleaning woman, are all for *Espagne.* Yes, your comrade was here and had a wonderful time. He left about fifteen minutes ago."

When they heard the word *Espagne,* the women stopped giggling and talking and sat as if waiting for an explanation. The madam turned to the women there, and, in French of course, told them who we were. As she talked, the hands of the two who were actively teasing me stopped for a moment. Then they moved again, this time in much more gentle, caressing motions. The rest of them sat up and clapped their hands and called out to us, *"Vive Espagne! Vive Espagne!"*

The madam then said to the two of us, "You must know how much we respect you. Anything you want here in our place, any of the girls would be proud and honored to serve you in any way. Without charge of course!" Her response seemed to me to be a combination of respect for the cause and a maternal caring for two who would face such danger.

Blushing, conflicted, and confused, I sputtered out "Thank you" and got out of there as fast as I could run. Hal followed me somewhat reluctantly.

When we returned to our billets, John was there and stood looking at us with a very superior smirk. I can't remember ever being so angry, so frustrated. He had violated instructions, he had once again put me in a position of having to assume the role of leader without the authority to back it up. His unrestrained urges had put him at risk of venereal disease and thus had made him a potential medical liability. And, at the same time, I was envious because of my own unfulfilled sexual desires. I was so enraged that I was afraid I would attack him if I said a word. So I brushed passed him and went up to our room to get some distance and could cool off. From then on my relations with him were as distant as I could make them.

A few hours after our return, word came that we were to move forward. We took public buses to the Gare de Lyon and boarded third-class coaches on the 7:30 train south to the city of Carcassonne, which is just north of the Spanish border. With additions from various European countries—Austrians, Brits, Belgians, Danes, Dutchmen, Slavs, Swedes, and escapees from German concentration camps—our number had increased to ninety-three.

Those who had gone earlier, before the Non-Intervention Pact had closed the border, had been able to take the train all the way into Spain and openly boast of their destination. They were greeted along the way by French farmers working in the fields who saluted them with arms raised and fists clenched. After the government crackdown, that was no longer possible. On this train the scenario was farcical low comedy. We were all pretending to be students or tourists who didn't know each other. No one carried a suitcase or pack. Here we were, ninety-odd young men, mostly in our early twenties, dressed similarly, wearing berets, crowded into a couple of railroad cars. Like the others, I had a small package with personal belongings and a paper bag with cheese and ham in a croissant, a banana, and an apple.

We studiously avoided looking at each other. Sig and I sat on the same bench but pretended to be strangers. While for the most part we kept up the pretense, every once in a while I would see one or another of the volunteers, contrary to orders, break discipline and whisper into the ear of his seatmate. I had a mixture of reactions. I wanted to laugh at all the pretense because it was so ridiculous. I was mad at those that broke the discipline that all the rest of us followed so scrupulously. Most of all, I was frightened that they would give away who we were and that we would be arrested. The wooden bench was uncomfortable, and there was no room to stretch out. On top of it all, I was so keyed up with the idea of actually being on my way that it was hardly possible to sit still and rest, let alone doze. The night seemed to go on forever.

CHAPTER
4

Carcassonne to Albacete

When the train squealed to a stop in Carcassonne shortly after daybreak the next morning, we dispersed into the little park around the station—that is, if ninety young men could be said to disperse in such a small space. It was a long, narrow, grassy strip in front of the station with a number of benches and a few trees. As directed, I took my group to the second farthest of the benches and then we sat waiting for someone to give directions. That my group looked to me for guidance made it worse. I had nothing to offer by way of information or reassurance, not even a Carcassonne contact. I hoped that Fred had backup information, just in case. I could only sit and wait as impatiently as the others, but certainly more anxiously.

After a short wait, a guide started his passes. Wearing the yellow sweater that was his identification, he made the agreed-upon hand signal of recognition—a clenched right fist held near his pants pocket. The interval of his appearances was about fifteen minutes. Fortunately, we were the second group, and so the torment was not so prolonged for us. One by one, each group of five or ten of us followed him, each man, at fifteen-foot intervals, pretending that he was just walking along the street, not part of a group, that the others were not following him.

If Carcassonne hadn't had a communist city administration and a sympathetic population, it would have been not only ludicrous but tragic as well. In this period, in addition to the regular border guards and nonintervention patrols at the boundaries seeking out volunteers, in some cities the local police were arresting the volunteers, and in some, pro-fascist gangs were attacking our comrades. Here I suspect that word had been put out to the community to ignore us. So there were few pedestrians on our winding route along the narrow cobblestone streets through town. Those few people we saw walked close to the buildings with their gaze averted, studiously avoiding seeing us.

By midmorning, our guide had collected all the groups. We were crowded into the second story of a small restaurant owned by a local Communist party member. The room was not big, perhaps thirty by forty feet. Everything movable, the portable bar and the few chairs and tables that were used for private parties, had been pushed against the walls, with the chairs stacked on top. To the right of the entrance was a small sink and drainboard. A couple of travel posters on the wall, one a scene of Leningrad, the other of Barcelona, were the only decorations. Two windows faced out to the street in front. The toilet was downstairs in the back of the restaurant; we could go to it without being seen by regular customers. At night we lay down in rows on the wooden floor, close to each other. In this room we spent the rest of that day, that night, and the following day without baths, showers, or hot water for shaving. During the day, we rolled up the blankets given to us and placed the stacked chairs back around the room.

We had expected to leave on our trip over the mountains into Spain the night of our arrival. But as soon as we were assembled in this room we were told that wasn't to be. We were not given any indication of what was delaying us or when we'd be able to depart. Tension grew. From time to time during our stay of almost forty hours, someone would appear at the second-floor door and say something in French about where the toilets were, when we would be fed, what we were to do, or what we weren't allowed to do. Frequently these announcements were poorly translated or there would be a squabble about what had been said.

"Be quiet, he said."

"No, he said that we weren't to sing too loudly."

"So what's the difference?"

"Stay away from the windows, don't let yourself be seen from the street."

"No, he said it was OK to be at the window."

These directives never came from the same person twice, nor did they seem to be very authoritative. Often it was a waiter who had been sent to deliver a message he didn't always understand himself. We were worried. Who was in charge? Was it safe? We had heard about volunteers being arrested or attacked. We heard rumors that those arrested were being mistreated, that other Brigaders were beaten to death by fascist gangs, or that German and Austrian volunteers were being turned over to Nazis agents and spirited back to concentration camps.

The delay, the uncertainty, the lack of information, and the crowding led to bickering over such unimportant things as who would sleep where. Was our sleeping position to be determined by nationality? If so, which group had the position by the windows? Was it to be a head-to-toe layout, or head-to-head? How much space between us? And so on endlessly. Each of us had been given a thin blanket. It was the first time many of us had ever slept on a hard floor.

With the resilience of youth, most of us managed without too much discomfort. But often I had to remind myself not to complain. Those of us who had sailed together now recognized Fred as our leader and tried to follow his lead as he tried to settle the various arguments. Some of the national groups, who either had no leaders or whose leadership was very weak, objected to everything. Outside of our own group, Fred's intervention didn't seem to help very much. Although the bickering was not too serious, it was annoying that we weren't united, a group acting in concert toward a single goal.

In the morning, before the restaurant was open, we went downstairs for breakfast. The front blinds, lowered when the restaurant had closed for the night, were still down. We were given the traditional French morning meal, which wasn't much, just coffee, which I never liked, and a sweet roll. At midday, waiters brought up a lunch of sandwiches with cold cuts and fruit.

We, the Americans and Canadians, joked and laughed a lot. One of our comrades was an excellent mimic, and he would give us fits portraying the immigration official who had taken so long to stamp each passport or the self-important Pierre who had been in charge of our Paris barracks. As a result, while we were the largest single national group of volunteers, many of the European volunteers saw us as happy-go-luckies who really didn't know what fascism was like and, therefore, were not serious in our commitment. They told us that we hadn't suffered, that we were too bourgeois, that our life in America was too easy. We tried to take into account what they had gone through in their home countries, but we were angry at being belittled, and the tension level escalated. We may not have suffered as they had, but many of us had been jailed and beaten during strikes or political actions. For many of our group, life hadn't been that easy. For my part, I felt that I had volunteered to put my life on the line just as much as they had, so I couldn't understand what they were they bitching about. Life, it seemed to me, didn't have to be so sober.

Once, when I was recounting to some comrades from England the incident of the pro-Hitler man on the balcony in Paris, I put my finger over my lip to signify a Hitler mustache and thrust out my right arm in salute and cried, a couple of times, "Heil Hitler, Heil Hitler!" A couple of the Germans, who didn't know what I was doing, became livid with anger, yelling *"verdammte fascist"* (damned fascist!).

I turned to them in bewilderment, trying to explain. "Look, comrades, I was telling a story about a French Nazi in Paris. Do you think I would be here if I loved Hitler?"

Both of them had become so enraged that either they couldn't hear me or couldn't understand my explanation. The two of them had to be physically restrained from attacking me. I later found out that they had suffered enormously at the hands of some sadistic guards in the concentration camp from which they had escaped and could see no humor in the charade. But at that moment, all I could see was that they were lacking a sense of humor.

The first night, those of us who spoke English had a bull session on what was happening in Europe. There were a considerable number of Europeans in the group who could speak English, including Germans who knew intimately what was occurring in Germany and Italy and had a deep understanding of the political situation in the various countries. They answered a lot of our questions, making real a lot of what we had only read about. I listened wide-eyed to hear firsthand an explanation of many of my political questions, to hear the reality of the terror that back in Los Angeles we could talk about only in generalities.

We learned that because the borders of France were closed, planes, trucks, and cannon bought by the Republic were stacked up near the frontier. Various countries had closed down credit sources, preventing the government from using its own money to buy what it needed. Loyalist bank accounts located in foreign lands, particularly those in Paris, were frozen. The Non-Intervention Pact had not, however, prevented the German and Italian governments from sending arms and troops by ship, landing them in huge quantities at the port of Cadiz in southern Spain. Italian submarines were active both in the Mediterranean Sea and in the Atlantic Ocean off the coast of Portugal, attacking and sinking ships with supplies headed either to the northwestern Loyalist areas of the Asturias and Basque regions or to the east to Barcelona and Valencia. Soviet ships, the main supply source for the Republic, had been torpedoed. Franco's air force and tank corps were staffed mainly by German personnel. Most of the Italian troops had been transferred to Spain in intact units in battalion or division size directly from fighting in Ethiopia or Abyssinia.

During the days, a few of us were let out in pairs to explore the city, which housed the ancient ruins of the famous medieval Carcassonne castle. The castle sat on the hill dominating the city, and we could see the huge fortress walls from the restaurant windows. Since there didn't seem to be any system for selecting the lucky pairs to go out, this became another source of friction. Every hour or so one of the waiters would ask who wanted to go. Almost everyone raised his hand. He would point to a couple of guys and say, "You may go." I was not one of the lucky ones. Those of us who stayed behind were envious.

For most of us the boredom was hard, and time passed very slowly. The guys who had been allowed out came back and told of what they had seen. Although that helped pass the time, I became even more envious. Around five, the waiters brought up dinner. This meant that they brought ninety-three plates, silverware and napkins, and big pots of food. It was some kind of meat and rice dish with some vegetables in it. The small kitchen was limited in what it could do because the preparation for us was in addition to their regular service.

The food wasn't bad; in fact, it was quite good. It was my introduction to French food, even if it was not three-star. I was hungry, as always, so I ate everything that was on my plate. Quite a few of my American comrades just poked at their food, whether because of their own tensions or because of the strangeness of the dishes I don't know. Afterward, we stacked the dishes onto some big metal trays, and the waiters came and cleared the room.

During the time we were there, the restaurant was always crowded at mealtimes, and the diners downstairs often seemed to be having loud political arguments. Around eleven o'clock on the second night, after the customers had all gone from the restaurant, we were loaded into a series of small buses and taxicabs, a few at a time. The buses all had their curtains drawn shut. Our departures were spaced far enough apart so as not to form, or at least to minimize, the appearance of a convoy on the road, which might have attracted unwanted attention. I drew one of the taxis, which held five of us. As group leader, I got to sit in front. John, as the youngest, had to sit on the floor in back. In this odd conglomeration of vehicles we rode an hour or so south, always along back roads to avoid notice. After about a half hour, the flat roads were left behind and we began to climb high into the foothills of the Pyrenees.

Soon we were traveling along a narrow, unmarked, and isolated road until there weren't even any farmhouses to be seen. Finally, the cab stopped and, in the darkness, the driver pointed off to our right. Carrying packages of food that had been issued to us at the restaurant, we walked a couple of hundred yards off the road to the ruins of a castle, where we were to spend the next twenty or so hours.

What was left of the castle were mainly crumbling stone walls, but we slept in the one large room that still had part of a roof over it that offered some protection from the night dew. Wrapping ourselves in the blankets that had been left by the previous contingent of volunteers, we lay down on the stone floor without any argument about who should sleep where. The internal tensions of the group seemed to have disappeared magically.

Finally, we were on the last lap of the journey to which we had looked forward for so long. All that was left was anticipation, plus some worry about what might happen on the way. But that worry was not directed against other comrades. All the next day we lay around. Some of us did pushups or other exercises to relieve our boredom, but there wasn't much else to do.

The man in charge, René, a Frenchman who did not stay with us, spoke some English and German. He explained that the purpose of the extra day back at the restaurant and this day at the castle was to make sure that at least one of the pair of guards patrolling in the area we would pass through would be sympathetic to us. This was the edge we needed to avoid arrest.

If we wanted to walk around during the day, we could, but it had to be up in the hills behind the ruins, so that we were well away from the road, hidden from any passersby. Actually, our location was so isolated that during the entire day we didn't see any people or vehicles passing. Finally, toward evening, René came back with a small truck and driver, bringing us our last French-side meal. The two of them stayed with us into the early evening, until we started our climb into Spain.

After eating, we folded and stacked our blankets, policed the area, and took the refuse and containers out to the truck, both for sanitation and to avoid attracting any attention. We left the blankets hidden in a small crypt within the ruins, to be used by the next group. When all had been cleaned up, we waited tensely for the orders to go on to Spain.

A few minutes after it was fully dark, two guides showed up to lead us in our trek over the mountains. They simply appeared, having walked down from the hills. As smugglers all their lives, they apparently knew every foot of these peaks intimately, where and how to move so that they would not be seen by guards or police. These two men were in their fifties, their hair and beards gray and their faces wrinkled. But those were their only signs of age, for they were unbelievably surefooted and strong.

We marched out of the castle happy to leave the tedium behind and to be moving again. Single file, we moved very quickly, first through a broad meadow that sloped only slightly up the hill. Soon the path changed to a very narrow, unmarked track with a sharp climb that began to slow us down a little. The guides pushed us hard. Even that little loss of speed brought forth commands of *"Vite! Vite! Vite!"* Pierre had told us that if we were caught on the French side in daylight, not even a sympathetic patroller could help us. Our two guides made the climb look easy, sometimes trotting ahead to scout for patrols, sometimes trotting back to push stragglers. For the rest of us, the climb was hard and scary.

Often the narrow path was on the edge of a gorge that appeared so precipitous that a misstep would have meant falling to a certain death. I was wearing ordinary, leather-soled street shoes, as were most of the Americans. They were lousy for mountain hiking. The soles had little traction on rocks that were often slippery from dew, and the oxford cut meant no support for my ankles. I constantly seemed to have to retie the laces, as the climbing and hiking kept loosening them. Two or three times they broke, and then I'd have to tie the parts back together. Groups that came later told us that they were given *alpargatas* (rope sandals) to wear, which was much more sensible.

Our instructions had been to keep silent under all circumstances, not even to sneeze. As there was no moon, the darkness within the enclosing mountain walls became so dense at times that we often had to depend on hearing the breathing of the man ahead of us for guidance. The sound of breathing, the slap of shoes, and men farting because of the exertion and the altitude—these were our guides.

Twice during the night an alarm was whispered down the line. The man in front of me softly passed the word, and excitedly I whispered "Patrol! Get down!" to the comrade following me. As instructed before we had started, we immediately went to the side of the path, where we flopped, hiding in the bushes or grass and maintaining absolute silence until the all clear was given.

Fortunately, both times this occurred, either by chance or by the planning of our guides, we were not on the narrowest portion of the trail, so there was room for us to get a few feet away from the path and hide. We lay down flat so that our faces wouldn't reflect light from the lanterns or flashlights of the patrol. I crooked my arm under me and put my head on it. Once, the mustiness of the soil almost made me sneeze, and I bit my lip until it bled trying to suppress it. The other time, my face was on a jagged rock that pressed hard into my cheek, so that it felt like it was cutting me. When the patrol actually was near me, I held my breath until they had passed, worrying that they would hear the frightened pounding of my heart.

One time, the threat had come from French border guards, the other time from a League of Nations Non-Intervention patrol. The job of the border guards was their normal boundary responsibility: to stop smuggling, prevent illegal entry, and, only incidentally, to stop us. The League patrol's only job was to stop us, with bullets if necessary. I was so angry about the whole Non-Intervention farce that I felt that I would willingly have shoved them off the precipice if they had tried to stop us.

Our delay of the extra days at the restaurant and at the castle apparently paid off in terms of a sympathetic patrol. I suppose that if we had been too obvious, even with their understanding views, they would have had to take some action against us. In the dark we lay there, hoping that we were well enough concealed, holding ourselves tightly together as they went by. Chatting, smoking their cigarettes, the patrol duets ambled along, taking their time. Fortunately, these guards, either deliberately or by chance, were without the guard dogs that we had been told so many of the patrols used. These pauses should have given us a chance to rest our muscles, but our tenseness from worrying about being caught made it impossible to relax. After the patrol had passed far enough off so that they couldn't hear us, our guides gave the signal and we struggled to our feet and started again, going perhaps a bit faster to make up for the moments lost.

The route was up, followed by more up.

From time to time I would think I saw the top ahead, and the joy at ending the climb would bring a surge of energy, until I saw more mountains hidden behind a false summit. Sometimes I would relax and smile to myself, thinking that we had it made because we were starting downhill. But after a few minutes down the path we would start climbing again, more often than not on an even steeper grade.

Get to the border by sunrise, get to the border!

I was in good health, even if not in great physical condition, and made the trip only minimally stressed, suffering a few muscle aches, shortness of breath, and now and then giving forth with a few grunts and groans, but able, nevertheless, to do the job without great strain. There were a few, mainly Germans and Austrians, who were conditioned mountaineers, who had proper footwear and for whom it was a breeze. But they had to help those who couldn't make it on their own.

Ed, who had started with me in Los Angeles, was in agony most of the way. At one point, more than halfway along the journey, he just gave up, lay down, and quit. I hadn't been aware of his pain until then, only that he was struggling almost from the beginning and seemed more awkward than most as we climbed.

When I went to him, he wheezed, "Let me alone, I can't go any farther."

"What's the matter, Ed?"

"I've got arthritis from the clap and both my knees have given out."

"I'm not going to let you die on this path. Come on, come on, you've come this far!" I reached for his shoulder. "I'll help you and together we can make it, we can't have too much farther to go."

Finally, ignoring his protests, I pulled him up and put my shoulder under his left armpit, grabbed his hand, and stretched his arm around my right shoulder and held it with my hand. We started the climb again. Together we stumbled along. Luckily, the path was broad at that point. He tried to control the moaning from his pain, I tried to control the wheezing from my effort. Fortunately, one of the Austrians soon came by and took over for me, making it seem effortless. In the remaining climb, one or another of the Austrians or Germans spelled each other. Annoyed and ashamed because of my limited physical strength, and also envious, I vowed to make myself stronger and get into tougher physical condition.

An agonizing time later, the false dawn lightened the sky just a little as we passed the unmarked border. There, on what seemed to be the top of the world, a Spanish guide sat on a rock, his black beret perched at an angle, smoking a cigarette, smiling a relaxed welcome.

"Bennvenet a Espania." Welcome to Spain.

Our two guides of the night gave us a quick, silent, farewell salute and started at a dogtrot back to their homes in France, looking as if they had merely been out for a short evening stroll with their families. Our new guide slowed our rate and let us rest frequently. There was little climbing now as we seemed to wander between peaks instead of having to climb them. I welcomed this change to an easier pace, but even so after a little while my knees began to stiffen and I began to feel my joints and muscles creak and ache.

As the first break in the darkness came and the sky began to lighten, the blackness of the mountain walls began to fade. I began to absorb the massiveness, the awesome beauty and strength of the Pyrenees, and I could begin to understand how Spain had such a unique character. This mountain chain stretching east to west all along the border was an absolute barrier that sealed the Iberian peninsula from the rest of the continent. I could see nothing but more mountain peaks in every direction. It was a strange and alien world with little life except an occasional dark-feathered hawk soaring in the distance. There was little growth, even though we were below the tree line. Dull browns and greens in various muted patterns colored the slopes. Mostly there were low-lying shrubs and patches of dried grass. The sheer grandeur of this mountain chain was overwhelming.

We had an hour or so of slow marching without climbing or descending, during which even Ed could make it alone, although one of the Austrians always walked beside him. Finally, we looked down on a little village below called Set Cases (Catalan for Seven Houses), the end of our mountain journey. In fact, the community was a little larger than that, having grown to more than a dozen or more homes since it was first named, who knows how many decades earlier. From above, it seemed miles away, but actually it was probably only a third of a mile, down a 30 or 40 percent grade.

We made a bouncy, aching descent to where trucks were to take us to the collecting center in the nearby city of Figueras. Some men rushed down the slope, some slid, others barely crawled, helping one another, but it was a happy, laughing group of men who scrambled down that mountainside. Not having the responsibility for Ed, who was being helped, down I went, jolting, half running, part sliding in elation at having reached my goal. What utter relief that I had finished the climb, that I had finally arrived in Spain, that I could be a part of the army that was going to end the fascist threat.

We sat alongside the road that ended at Set Cases and were handed something to eat and drink by some of the villagers, who seemed used to foreigners coming down their mountain and welcomed us with smiles. We waited, lying on the ground, for about a half hour, until a small convoy came for us. On command, we climbed into these canvas-covered army trucks. Many of the men collapsed inside, exhausted. I, with a few others, stayed by the open end of our truck, hoping to see this new country and to greet and be greeted by the Spaniards we would pass on the road, to express our joy at arriving, to demonstrate our feelings of solidarity. Much to our surprise and disappointment, there was to be no opportunity to celebrate, to punctuate our arrival, for the order came to drop the canvas flaps of the truck and be quiet.

In May, just a few weeks before our arrival, there had been an uprising in Catalonia against the central government. While the revolt had been quickly put down without a great deal of strife, apparently Madrid felt that showing more foreigners coming to the army would signal to the local population a strengthening of the central government and roil a still tense and uncertain political situation.

In my naïveté, it was quite a shock to realize that the Republic was not a unified nation, that there could be a separatist movement active at this time when the nation was threatened. I suppose I had expected everybody who was against Franco to be for the central government, for the Republic.

Through the past centuries, the Catalonian region had fought repeatedly to maintain and at other times to achieve its independence—from Rome, from Spain, and from France. In the last centuries, the fight had been against Madrid, which at various times had suppressed the Catalan language and its culture and outlawed its political organizations.

A central struggle of the Catalan uprising stemmed from the feeling of a large segment of the workers that they first had to win the workers' revolution before the job of putting down the Franco forces could be done. These anarchists, who were a major political component of the Catalan working class, not only wanted regional freedom but in addition wanted no government other than self-governing local trade unions, neighborhood groups, or regional associations. The rest of the workers and a large part of the population supported the central government in Madrid. Those included the socialists, the communists, and the Republicans.

For most of us, it seemed incomprehensible that winning the war wasn't the first job for everyone in the Republic. Most of the story of discontent that I had read back home, I guess, I had dismissed as fascist propaganda. I knew nothing about anarchism. I had never knowingly met or talked to an anarchist and knew them only as the spectral figures portrayed in cartoons as bewhiskered, short, fat, round, sleazy men with hats on their heads and round bombs with sputtering fuses in their hands. Now, of course, I quickly learned the struggle against fascism was much more complex, that it was possible to be antifascist from a variety of political positions.

The trucks carried us to an ancient fort in the modern city of Figueras, which was about twelve miles south of the French border. Cut into a hill in the thirteenth century, it was two-thirds underground, with twenty-foot-thick earthen walls. Its massiveness, which had stood off the repeated onslaughts of Napoleon's army, was not apparent from the outside. The entrance was through a huge arch thirty feet high and wide enough to allow passage of two cars. Now its heavy wooden doors were swung back, but there were manned machine guns at the entrance.

We walked deep into the belly of the fort. As we did, the realization of having finally arrived hit me. Even if I had wanted to, there was no longer the option of turning back. Now I was no longer a group leader but just another soldier-to-be. We were checked in with a minimum of paperwork, our arrival recorded, and then we were directed down a flight of stone stairs to one of the fort's cavernous rooms. There, cots were neatly laid out with blankets carefully folded. We joined other recruits who had crossed the border a few days or even a week or so before us. The army was waiting for enough men to arrive from abroad to justify allocating a train from its limited reserves to take us down to the center of Spain, where the headquarters of the International Brigades was located. The fort seemed large enough to house an entire city, with its many levels and corridors that seemed to extend for miles. Many of the walls were covered with the names of those who had passed through here, probably from wars long past.

During the day, they took us outside onto a flat area near the entrance of the fort and started some rudimentary marching and drilling instruction. Such a mixup! The drill instructors, who came from among the volunteers, had been selected only because they had confessed to some previous military experience, which may have been only as a clerk or truck driver. They knew nothing about giving marching commands. Also, language difficulties made it frustrating on both sides—those hearing the commands and trying to execute them, and those trying to give them. Unlike our multilingual bickering in Carcassonne, here we mixed without friction, with friendship, and even with a great deal of laughter at our clumsy attempts at marching together. Now that we were in Spain to do what we had come for, it seemed we could put up with difficulties.

After dinner, there were the inevitable bull sessions. We Americans told of the organizing struggles of the workers and students, and about some of the violent events that had occurred during political demonstrations. But the stories we heard from Europeans left us awed and angry, for they were even more immediate and personal that those we had listened to back in that crowded room above the restaurant in Carcassonne. To hear firsthand the stories of those who had spent time in prison camps and escaped, or the horror of what it was like to have lived under Nazi rule, was enough to make us stronger in our commitment to defeat Franco and thus rebuff Hitler and Mussolini. Their stories made anti-Semitism and fascism real in a way that it had been impossible for me, coming from an atmosphere of mild and polite discrimination, to grasp.

One of the men who had threatened to attack me at the Carcassonne restaurant told, through the translation of one of his German comrades, of the daily, routine beatings on the soles of his feet administered by two of his camp guards because he would not salute them in what they considered a proper and respectful manner. Others told of how their families had been torn apart, many being taken to different concentration camps where they were worked or starved to death. Or how they had been forced from their homes, their businesses confiscated; how they were attacked on the street by uniformed storm troopers while the police stood by, watching with smiles on their faces.

Although I had never thought of myself as worldly, listening to my European comrades made me understand how little I knew of real evil, how shallow was my understanding of what men could do to one another.

The next day, as we were marching, Erik, a volunteer from Bulgaria, and I became friends, a friendship that started just as we smiled at each other. I'm not sure what really attracted me to him; I knew only that he had the most engaging smile I'd ever seen and also that he seemed as eager to perform well as I. That night, instead of going to one of the bull sessions, the two of us went to a cafe. He spoke no Spanish and no English and just a little German. I spoke no Spanish and no Bulgarian and just a little German. Unfortunately, the German words that I had learned in high school were not always the same ones he knew, and vice versa. But somehow, with the few words we shared, the exchange of photographs, with gestures and with lots of goodwill, we managed to communicate. We sat and drank cheap brandy, eventually getting quite drunk by the end of the evening. We told each other deep secrets about our lives, our wants, our failures, our loves. At least I did, and I think he did also. We laughed, cried, sang together, and established a warm comradeship. He showed me pictures of his parents and two sisters, his home, the dog he had left behind. He was going to be a dentist when this war was over.

All of this was conveyed in sign language. For dentist he bared his teeth, made his finger into a drill, made a buzzing sound, and then pointed to himself. He explained his plan to marry by putting a ring on his finger. He talked about his country, drawing maps and showing where his hometown was. He said that after Franco (a word we both knew) was defeated (a gun to Franco's head), he would fight for freedom in his homeland (a gun firing while pointing to his home on the map). I spoke of the problems with my father (papa was a word he understood) and made fists like a boxer. I told of missing my close friends Al, Jack, Lorraine, and Ruth. I drew maps to show him where Los Angeles is. I told of my dreams of becoming a famous novelist or perhaps a bacteriologist who would discover cures for terrible diseases, of wanting a woman to love. I don't know how much of what I tried to say he understood, how much of his talk I was able to grasp. Somehow we understood each other. Sometimes deep bonds between two men are established without a real exchange of words. In this case, just an inchoate sharing of feelings, of a need brought on by a combination of fear and hope. I'm not sure how deep it was, but I felt that it was real, not just the brandy, not only the loneliness and the fear of what might happen to us in the near future.

Several days at the fort stretched out to almost a week. Then we left aboard a special train for central Spain. It went south and east to Barcelona and then, without stopping in the city, down the Mediterranean coast toward Valencia. After we passed by the southern border of Catalonia, where the Ebro River enters the sea, we no longer were required to be silent. We could lean out windows and shout slogans and yell greetings as we pleased. It was thrilling that our greetings were returned with enthusiasm and with clenched-fists salutes. That made up for our silent passage from Paris to Figueras.

We made several stops along the way at small stations as we yielded the track to trains with more urgent cargo. At each of these stops we were welcomed by the railroad workers as well as by people who were there waiting for their transportation. Once, three young girls happened to be in the station as we stopped, and they gave us a couple of small sacks of oranges they were carrying, crying *"Viva Los Internacionales!"* A wonderful introduction to the center of Spain.

CHAPTER
5

Albacete

Just north of Valencia, our train changed directions, switching away from the ocean to go west. It left the Mediterranean coast and started climbing up onto Spain's central plateau and heading for the little city of Albacete, the center of Cervantes's La Mancha country, where we detrained. It was a dreary, small city whose only claim to fame before the war had been its boast that it was the "saffron center of the world." Its main streets were cobblestoned, many of the side streets unpaved—a small town of mainly single-story buildings, all of them displaying the same drab architecture. Now, refugees, Spanish army personnel, and the headquarters of the International Brigades had swollen the city to more than twice its peacetime population.

Located a hundred miles or so from the front, it was just at the edge of bombing range, which in those days was quite limited. Consequently, it suffered only three limited bombings during the entire war. Albacete was the only city in the La Mancha area that, at the outbreak of the revolt, had been captured and held by the Guardia Civil (the Civil Guard, or police, who were loyal to Franco). They were in control for only a couple of days before a gathering of trade unionists in the city and peasants from the surrounding area stormed their barracks and drove them out.

We were formed into a column six across and given the command to march. Some of us tried in an awkward way, but most just walked and talked, sometimes three abreast, sometimes eight, or clumped into groups. It would be a while before we would learn to march in order and to take it seriously. All along the dusty street, brightly colored posters and banners nailed to the walls or hung from ropes strung across the street called for support of the war effort and saluted the Brigades Internacionales. People on the street greeted us warmly with smiles and cries of *"Viva,"* and many saluted us. It was all very festive—like a big party, not a disciplined organization, certainly not the picture of men grimly going to battle.

Before we went to the nearby headquarters of the International Brigades to be formally enrolled in the army, we were taken to the bull ring. There we were separated into groups by language, each group distant enough from the others to ensure that those who addressed us would not disturb those speaking to the adjoining groups. First came a welcome speech, much more like a canned pep talk. Then others spoke, giving us information about Spain, the government, the army, and our enemy.

We were told a little about the brief history of the Republic and the Revolt of the Generals, now a year old. The speaker told us the names of the heads of government and the leaders of the army. I forgot them almost as fast as he rattled them off. The constitution, he said, was even more conservative than ours in the United States. In no way could Spain be considered a communist or socialist country. The elected Cortes (parliament) had initiated some land reform, built public schools, separated church and state, and established a democratic form of government. While it seemed tame to me, it was apparently quite radical for Spain.

Then he spoke of the many changes since the advent of the Republic. Before the war, in Madrid, a city of 1,800,000 inhabitants, 300,000, or one in six, had been servants. This caste system had also been reflected in the military, where there was one general for every 150 enlisted men and 21,000 officers for 130,000 rank and file, also one in six. It was a ratio of officer to enlisted personnel higher than that found in any other major army.

With the revolt, the overwhelming majority of the armed forces, particularly the officer corps, sided with Franco. The Republican army was left without a trained and experienced leadership. Those few officers who remained loyal frequently were regarded with suspicion as possible double agents. Often, therefore, their capabilities were not fully utilized.

The former pervasiveness and authority of the church was difficult for an American to comprehend. There had been twenty thousand monks, sixty thousand nuns, and thirty-one thousand priests. In most respects it was a fossilized organization that had refused to change in almost any detail. Protestants were considered "dammed souls." The Catholic Church, centered in Rome, was very conservative and even often rigid. It had survived century after century throughout the world because of its ability to adapt to new world conditions, but that was not true in Spain, where inflexibility was the norm.

Church law in the nation was absolute, yet the Spanish people showed their partial separation from its dictates in the way they reacted to the institutional church. They had a profound spirituality, a somewhat fanatical faith in their attachment to their religion, yet that was combined with a virulent anticlericalism. Surveys in the 1930s showed that two-thirds of the population would not be regarded as practicing Catholics. While the church was involved in their weddings, baptisms, and funerals, the majority of Spaniards did not go to confession or to Mass. Of those who did practice their religion, women were the main group, with old men the next largest segment.

When the government stripped away the church's authority over secular issues, many cathedrals and churches were burned or trashed and many priest beaten, some killed. In some instances, this was an expression of local rage against the restraints of church doctrine. More often, it was simply anger against the repressive actions and arrogance of individual local priests.

Furthermore, when these outbreaks occurred, at the same time the police force of the Republic had largely disappeared from their stations, so there was no organized force available to put down the violence. The delays in reestablishing public order came from political struggles for control and resulted in considerable terrorism, not only against the clergy but also against supporters of right-wing parties, and sometimes against ordinary citizens in the execution of personal grudges. This lawlessness alienated many and slowed the unification of the nation. In addition, the unqualified support of the Vatican and the clergy for Franco made the decision about which side to support difficult for Catholics, for, despite their anticlericalism, the church still had a strong pull.

Perhaps the conflict between the church and the people of Spain is best expressed in the most common Spanish swear words. Almost all of them were denigrations or defamations of holy objects—such as talk of defecating or urinating upon, or otherwise defiling or defaming, the holy wafer, the holy Trinity, the holy mother, even the twenty-four balls of the twelve apostles. Later during my service, my driver, Pacho, when angry, would go around muttering *"Ostia, ostia,"* or "holy wafer, holy wafer." What he really was doing was shortening *"Me cargen la ostia,"* which meant "I defecate upon the holy wafer."

The status of women had changed with the new government as well. The church's extreme position on women was perhaps exemplified by its dictum that young girls must wear shirts when taking a shower in private, because water all over a woman's uncovered body was declared a sin. With the rule of the church terminated, abortion was legalized in Catalonia; centers for women were established that welcomed prostitutes and unmarried mothers; birth control information was made available; "marriage by usage" was recognized, meaning that couples who cohabitated for ten months were considered married, and such a marriage was recognized in less time if a pregnancy resulted. It was certainly not a complete liberation. Women still washed clothes and did the cooking and raised the children, besides working in outside jobs. But the atmosphere had changed. With men away in the army, the women often took over the running of factories as well as serving as officials in village governments.

On the rebel side, the army had virtually no true volunteers from other countries. A handful of men recruited and funded by the Catholic Church in Ireland, from the semi-fascist movement called the Blue Shirts, came in the early days of the revolt under General Eoin McDuffy. But they left six months later, griping about the heat and cold. Militarily they had not covered themselves with glory. A small band from France formed the Jeanne d'Arc Battalion (actually, less than a battalion in size), and there was a very small White Russian group led by General Anton Foch. Altogether, the total of all these volunteers was probably less than a thousand.

But the insurgents had a lot of "nonvolunteers." The Germans sent close to twenty-five thousand men altogether, of which about six thousand were present at any one time. Notable were their first-class pilots, together with their best heavy bombers, fighting planes, and maintenance personnel. Nazi tank companies, antiaircraft and heavy artillery batteries, all fighting with German equipment, served the rebel army. In addition, German officers and noncoms ran schools for Spanish officers-in-training, supervised the laying of mines, and instructed in the maintenance of equipment.

Spain was seen by the leaders of the German Wehrmacht as a wonderful training opportunity for wars yet to come, so there was a rapid turnover of their people. Once exposed to battle and having tested their military skills and equipment, the men were brought back to raise the quality of the German army. With the exception of the men from the Condor Legion of the Luftwaffe, whose aerial feats were boasted about, their presence was hidden or denied until the records were opened decades later at the Nuremberg Trials. Then the world clearly saw that these alleged volunteers had been under German command. Their salaries and expenses had been paid by the German government.

While the Germans denied complicity, Mussolini boasted of his contributions, especially when they were successful in battle. But after the Republican victory over the Italian forces at Guadalajara (largely by Italian volunteers on our side), Il Duce was so angry at their defeat that he roared that none of his "volunteers" could come back to Italy until they had achieved a victory. Captured Italian regular army soldiers spoke of being forced to volunteer under threat of severe punishment. Altogether, about a hundred thousand Italian regular troops saw duty in Spain, some as entire divisions sent directly from their stations in Abyssinia or Ethiopia.

On top of the direct intervention with matériel and troops, the closing of the French and Portuguese borders, combined with attacks on shipping by Italian submarines and planes, interdicted delivery of almost all supplies to the Republic. Moreover, much of the Republic's funds deposited in various foreign banks, such as the Bank of Paris, were frozen. (After the war, these funds were turned over to the Franco government.)

The United States, on its own, instituted and maintained an arms embargo. Not satisfied with that, it also put heavy pressure on Mexico, which was the only nation other than the Soviet Union helping the Republic, to stop sending supplies. The League of Nations was impotent in getting the Axis nations to adhere to the Non-Intervention pact. The Soviet Union was faced with its ships being sunk and borders being closed, and so supplies from there soon dwindled.

On the rebels' side, with the advent of war the military was preeminent in making the decisions of government and of warfare. While the soldiers got on with the job of winning the war, political differences were held in abeyance or at least minimized. The military was in tight control, their goals quite clear. They wanted to establish an authoritarian, corporate state, to destroy organizations of the working class, and to dismantle the institutions of democracy.

Mussolini made his decision to help Franco defeat the Republic early on and never deviated from his position, wanting another sympathetic nation in the Mediterranean. Hitler, on the other hand, was ambivalent at first. He did not want Franco to have a quick victory. But it was equally clear that he did not want the Republic to win. He wanted the war to continue, since several years of warfare would give him time to test his armaments and the tactics and strategies of his military forces. Dive bombing was one such tactic. The equipment he sent, particularly the artillery and heavy bombers, were the best of the war. His officer corps had the opportunity to learn what was effective and then bring that back to the Wehrmacht. Further, it gave him time to rearm with weapons modified after being tested in battle.

At the outbreak of the rebellion, Hitler's hold on his middle and upper classes was not yet complete. His cry of antibolshevism with regard to Spain became an effective rallying point for further solidifying the German nation behind him. And from a matériel point of view, he needed the tungsten, iron, and nickel from Spain's mines for making his weapons. Also, the war allowed Hitler to forge the German-Italian Axis, which was not formally established until October of 1936, four months after the outbreak of the rebellion.

On our side, international volunteers had started their trek to the battlefront almost from the first days of the revolt, a spontaneous joining in a struggle against fascism. Some just happened to be in Spain on vacation. Some were living there, having found refuge from the dictatorships in their homelands. The first foreign volunteer to be killed was an English woman, Felicia Brown, living at the time on the eastern coast of Spain. Among the first to enlist were those who had come to Barcelona for a Workers' Olympiad that had been scheduled to start July 20, just after the rebellion began. With the exception of a small group of Italian-American trade-union men, most of whom served with the Italian Garibaldi Battalion, volunteers from the United States arrived much later than others. The first ninety-six Americans sailed from New York the day after Christmas of 1936, a little more than five months after the war started.

There were probably never more than fifteen thousand serving in our International Brigades at any one time. This figure included medical workers and other noncombatants. Casualties and repatriations kept the numbers down. The French were the first to arrive in any numbers, and they could go back and forth across the French border with relatively few restrictions from either France or the Republic. No records were kept. Even later, when records were kept of how many came from each country, the information was confusing. For example, the count of Belgian volunteers was mixed up with that of the French because they spoke the same language. Also, many Poles who had volunteered while working in the French and Belgian mining areas were counted as French. There was so much intermingling of the early fighters that the 9th Battalion of the 14th Brigade was known as the Battalion of Nine Nationalities. So many French lost their lives in those early days that if one walked in the International Brigade Cemetery in Madrid and looked at the names on the grave markers, it looked like a street in Paris.

More than sixteen hundred of the early arrivals died in the first weeks of the defense of Madrid. Record-keeping in those days was as haphazard as was the formal organization of the fighting forces. In addition, at the end of the war many of the records were lost or destroyed. In 1993, nearly 100,000 documents were discovered in the Russian Center for the Preservation and Study of Modern History Documents. They had been trucked to the Soviet Union in 1939 to avoid capture by advancing Franco armies. These have just been made available to ALBA (the Abraham Lincoln Brigade Archives at Brandeis University) and are being microfilmed and sent to the United States.

Many of our volunteers from eastern Europe who showed up at the Parisian mobilization centers were refugees from fascist rule. To a large extent, they were men who felt they had nothing to lose. Just getting to Paris had been extremely difficult. The governments of Europe, particularly the right-wing ones of the Balkans and eastern Europe, attempted to halt the movement of these men to Spain, but they could, at most, only slow down the stream.

After February of 1937, it was illegal for inhabitants of countries that were signatory to the Non-Intervention Pact to go to Spain to fight. Switzerland made even the discussion of the Spanish struggle a penal offense. Belgium gave fifteen-year sentences to those caught in transit. The Copenhagen-Paris railroad became known as the "Red Express," because it was used to avoid travel through Germany. Josip Broz (later known as Marshall Tito) created a secret underground railway from the Balkans that went to Vienna and then to Zurich and Paris. In spite of help from local communists and other antifascist sympathizers, many men were arrested en route. The difficulties of getting to France were so great that sometimes it took as long as five months for many of them just to reach Paris. Sometimes they had to wait weeks in one location until local searches by the police ended. Other times they were delayed because sympathizers along the way needed time to raise the money necessary for train fares, bribes, or other expenses.

Men and women came to the Republic from fifty-three or fifty-four countries around the world, an intermittent stream that finally totaled almost forty-five thousand. When the fascists spoke of us in their public pronouncements, they exaggerated our numbers so as to inflate the idea of a Red Menace and thus create a propaganda screen with which to mask the enormous quantities of men and matériel Germany and Italy were sending.

There were few soldiers from the Soviet Union. Although the records show that there were some high-ranking officers from the Red Army, I personally remember seeing only seven or eight, who were in a tank corps. Some students of the USSR speculate that during the great purges in Russia of 1937–38 Stalin didn't trust many officers out of the country, for fear of their defection. So he sent mainly communists from neighboring countries, those with military backgrounds who were living in exile in the USSR.

Finally, when our orientation speeches were finished, we were taken to the headquarters. We filled out questionnaires about our backgrounds and provided the names of people to notify in case of death. Our work backgrounds were also taken, for any usable skills or specialties. Then we were enrolled. Our oath of allegiance had been carefully worded so that we would not be pledging allegiance to a foreign government and thus jeopardize our citizenship at home. Rather, we swore to follow the rules and regulations of the army. After giving my oath, I finally felt that I was a soldier, even though no one had handed me a rifle.

Next, our passports were gathered up. It was feared that if we were captured or killed with them on us, the fascists would turn them over to the Gestapo for use in getting their secret agents into other countries. A few men from central Europe refused to give theirs up, because they had had such a hard time getting them. Some had had to bribe officials or buy expensive forged documents; others had been forced to wait a very long time before their passports were issued. Despite the promise that our passports would be returned to us at the end of our service, the protesters, who included a few Americans, just didn't trust the bureaucracy. They were afraid, too, that the documents might be turned over to the Comintern for the placement of its agents. After a long and shouted argument that became very heated on both sides, the Brigade officials gave in and the few objectors were allowed to keep their passports.

With all the paperwork settled, we went next door to the *Intendencia,* or supply service. There we were issued clothes that passed for uniforms. The pants might be blue, the shirt khaki. Some had repairs of what looked like bullet holes. It seemed as if we were being given the surplus of several armies. Many of the articles had clearly been used before. Often they did not fit. We started circulating the clothes in a sort of swapping bee. If my issue pants were too small, then there was someone with others that were too large.

Berets were also given out to those who had none, but they were not all the same size, style, or color. Much to my surprise, I discovered that there were beret styles that varied from region to region. Shapes and sizes differed by occupation. Even how they were worn on the head told something about the wearer. Agricultural workers who worked outdoors in the sun formed their large berets into a protective visor or sloped them down to shield the back of their necks from the sun. City dwellers wore small berets on the top of the head, although in the rainy season they might replace them with larger ones to protect against the weather.

Later on, just before we moved to the front, we were issued steel helmets that had been made for the French army of World War I. They seemed almost paper thin, without liners, and were often so ill-fitting that they threatened to blow off in a strong wind. Many men didn't wear them, even in battle, for it didn't seem as if they could deflect either a bullet or a piece of shrapnel, and they weren't comfortable.

The shoes I had worn climbing the mountains had come apart. The issued pair were stiff, secondhand, ankle-high boots, with the leather of the inner soles crinkled in the wrong places. Fortunately, a couple of days later I was able to get some *alpargatas*. Unfortunately, the sandals gave only limited protection from rocks. In the first days, until the soles of my feet toughened, my feet were always sore. The best I could do was to limp along and try not to show my discomfort.

The other hardships we endured didn't bother me much, not even severe stress. I also tolerated the outer limits of heat and cold quite easily. There is a family story, buttressed by a photo, about one winter when I was four. I was with my father in the Chicago railroad station, waiting for the train to Milwaukee. I was running up and down the platform, which was piled with snow between the tracks, wearing short pants, a cap, and a short coat that left my legs uncovered. Someone complained to a policeman that this was dangerous to my health. The officer went up to my Dad to ask him to get warmer clothes for me. At that moment I came up to them, overheard some of the conversation about my needing more clothes, and cried out that I was too hot. I started to take off my overcoat.

After we dressed in military clothing, we were sorted into five brigades. The 11th Brigade was German speaking and called the Thaelmann;

the 12th Brigade was Italian speaking and named the Garibaldi; the 13th Brigade was Slavic speaking and called the Dombrowski. The 14th Brigade, the Franco-Belge, was French speaking and included some of the French-speaking Poles; the 15th Brigade was mainly English speaking.

In the 15th Brigade, which was a part of the 35th Division, there were four battalions. The first was the British, or Saklatvaka, Battalion, named after a Hindu member of Parliament from the London district. It was usually referred to as the "English Battalion" or just as the "Brits," although it included some Irish volunteers who were divided between that unit and the Lincoln Battalion. The British contingent was almost wiped out in one afternoon during the Battle of Jarama. The second was the newly activated Mackenzie-Papineau Battalion, named for an earlier Canadian prime minister, William Lyon Mackenzie, who had led an armed struggle together with Louis Papineau against the British forces occupying Canada. The third was the Spanish Battalion, composed of Cuban, Mexican, Puerto Rican, and South American volunteers. The fourth was the Abraham Lincoln Battalion. Later, another battalion was formed, the George Washington Battalion, which was eventually merged into the Lincolns after a high casualty rate in the Brunete Campaign had hit them both. This then became the Lincoln-Washington Battalion. As the war progressed and casualties decimated the ranks of these battalions, and as the influx of volunteers decreased, all of the international battalions began to incorporate a higher and higher percentage of Spanish troops.

CHAPTER
6

Tarazona de la Mancha

We Americans, Canadians, and British piled onto a couple of trucks and were driven to Tarazona de la Mancha, the headquarters for training English-speaking troops. This small town on the central plateau of Spain is about halfway between Madrid and Valencia. The area had some small, rolling hills but mostly it was flat, and during the summer this highland was very hot and dusty. The terrain was a mixture of olive groves, wheat fields, many vineyards, and some stands of pine trees. Most of the young men living here were away in the army, so the farming and work of the town was done mainly by the women and the older men of the village.

Our relationship with the townspeople was excellent. The men who had come for training before us had made special efforts to develop good relations with them. They had raised money by giving part of their pay to establish a school for the children of refugees, occasionally worked in the fields with the farmers, and even, every once in a while, contributed a day's rations of bread or beans. We kept up the tradition, and so they were warm and welcoming. Some of them could never quite understand that we came from America, and they kept calling us "Russos" no matter how often we tried to explain the difference.

Upon arrival, I was assigned to the just-activated Mackenzie-Papineau Battalion (later officially the 60th Battalion), which, in spite of being called the Canadian Battalion, was almost two-thirds American. Over a thousand Canadians served in the Brigades, despite the efforts of the King government to stop the nation's widespread agitation and support for the

Spanish Republic. Prime Minister King had made the issuance of passports very difficult, had a law passed instituting prison time for anyone fighting in a foreign war, and had the Canadian federal police actively intimidating pro-Loyalist individuals and groups. Most of the Canadian volunteers simply crossed the border into the United States and then shipped out from New York City.

Larry, the comrade in charge of training for the battalion, assigned each one of us to a company. The battalion was composed of one machine gun and three infantry companies, and I was posted to the machine gun company. When all the assignments had been made—that is, all but one—Larry turned to Bert, a volunteer from Philadelphia, and told him that he was the new battalion cook. Bert had listed cooking experience when we were registering back in Albacete.

Bert started yelling. "I came here to fight, not to stir shit over a stove."

"You'll be contributing just as much seeing that your comrades are fed as being on the firing line," said Larry, trying to calm Bert down.

"Why can't you get a local to do it? There must be cooks around. The Spanish know how to cook, don't they?"

"Because we need you. This will be your job. You can train some Spanish comrades as assistants, but we need someone competent not only to cook but also to plan and organize."

"What sort of a job is this to come all this way across the ocean and over the mountains for?"

"Look Bert, most of all we have to have someone who has the guts to see that the food gets delivered to the front under battle conditions. We also need someone who's both smart and tough and also has the know-how so that what we get is decent enough to eat."

Because we wanted to be fed well, the rest of us stood around and encouraged him to take the job. We wanted to be fed.

"Go for it, Bert."

"We need you."

"Go ahead, take it."

Larry's arguments, plus the encouragement from the rest of us, and the fact that in the army you take orders, finally overcame his agitated, prolonged protests. His selection turned out to be a good fit. Even though he wasn't a fancy cook, he fed us well. Hearing him bitch about the job at almost every meal, but also liking the food he prepared, the rest of us rarely made any criticisms of the kitchen for fear that he would get mad and quit.

After Larry agreed to become the battalion cook, we were taken to our barracks. There our company commander and his section leaders separated us into gun squads, each of which consisted of twelve men. We were assigned to positions, and I was made squad leader. The leader had the temporary rank of *sargento* (sergeant). Under the sergeant came the assistant leader, the *cabo* (corporal), who also fired the Maxim gun and whose primary responsibility was its care and cleaning. The number-three man fed the belts of ammunition during firing. Then came a couple of men who carried spare parts and extra belts and cartridges and who also reloaded the belts. The rest of the squad were riflemen whose primary job was to protect the gun during attack, especially if the gun jammed and couldn't fire. They also helped dig in and install and move the Maxim. In an emergency, they took over the gun itself. In fact, in battle our roles were often interchangeable as men were wounded or killed or other exigencies of battle made themselves felt.

I was both excited and worried about my new assignment. In celebration of the selection I tried to grow a mustache in order to look more mature, once again without success, for the sparse growth on my upper lip made me look even younger. I felt so intense a need to prove myself as a soldier that I lived in fear of not measuring up. At the same time, I had to clamp down on the desire to exercise my authority and strut a bit. I was also keenly aware that I was only *acting* head of the squad, which raised both my anxiety and also my determination to prove myself. Formal ranks were awarded only when the unit actually headed for the front, or, afterward, when leadership ability had been demonstrated in battle. The official announcement of promotions in a newly formed unit was a strong signal that active combat was just ahead. I wanted to keep my rank. Until formal promotions, everyone carried the official rank of *soldado* (soldier), the lowest rank.

Our heavy Russian Maxims had already been obsolete during World War I. Nevertheless, they were wickedly effective guns. These days, when I look at photographs of us standing behind our guns, they look so small that it seems we could have picked them up and carried them with one arm, as one would a young puppy. Instead, I remember them as huge pieces, almost the size of heavy artillery. They were 1914 vintage, built with thick iron wheels, a big, metal, water-cooled jacket, and a thick and heavy steel shield. Every part was heavy.

On paved or hard surfaces, the Maxims went along without too much trouble. But when we had to drag them across open fields, they sank heavily into the dirt or sand and seemed to weigh a ton and a half, so that, pulling them, I felt like an overburdened burro. Besides pulling the Maxim, I also carried a belt of ammunition, a cleaver-sized knife, a small shovel or pick, and a canteen of water. Over my shoulder I had my blanket, rolled bandolier fashion and tied with a piece of rope. Inside the blanket was a spare barrel for the Maxim plus a few personal items such as letters from home, razor, and soap. When the gun was in its firing position, the carriage had to be weighed down to minimize shaking and to keep it from veering off target. Consequently, the squad always had to carry empty sandbags, another bulky burden that slowed our pace.

After our daytime duties were done and dinner was finished, most of us retired to our barracks, carrying our precious Maxim up the stairs and placing it in the middle of the floor between the rows of bunks.

"Hey Larry, that was a big batch of letters you got today. How many women did you leave behind?"

"It should only be. Naw, one of the guys from my longshore local, my working buddy, organized the letter-writing and then did all the mailings at once. He has a gimpy leg so he couldn't come, even though he can do his job on the waterfront well. Did you hear that the ILWU got a good new contract without having to strike this time?"

As we relaxed, some, like Larry, wrote letters, some read, but many of us began to take care of our weapons. The machine gun squad also carried rifles, and so we had to learn that weapon as well. They too were well vintaged, some even carrying the insignia of the czar on the barrel.

"Did you hear that there was a big demonstration in Marseille? Seems like some guys heading for here got picked up and the cops beat them up, so the demo was in protest."

We would disassemble, clean, and reassemble our guns, often several times before lights were turned out. Most of the time I worked on the Maxim, taking the firing mechanism apart. The goal was to be able to strip our weapon, clean it, and put it back together again quickly—and so automatically that the operation could be accomplished in the dark or under battlefield conditions, if necessary. We also took the shield and carriage off and put them back together again so that, if necessary, three men could carry the gun up steep hills or across a stream.

"Let me have the oil can, I think I see a rust spot that needs to be worked out." As we were taking the guns apart, we gabbed about the day's happenings, told each other of news from home that had come in the mail, or talked about what we'd heard was happening in the world outside of Tarazona. Lights out was at 10:30, and we had no trouble sleeping until 5:30 reveille.

The most limited part of our training was on the target range, because there wasn't much ammunition. The first time there, I was given three cartridges—not three belts—for our heavy machine gun. To treat the Maxim as a rifle was almost impossible, for if I left my finger on the trigger a fraction of a second too long, all three cartridges would have been fired.

When the Lincoln Battalion first went into action in the defense of Madrid on February 27, 1937, they carried pre–World War II rifles for which they had had only five practice rounds. Day after day, over and over, we practiced setting up our guns, digging in, loading (with empty belts), and then pretend-firing. Toward the end of the training period they gave us more cartridges, so that we could actually learn how to fire the weapon as a machine gun and see if we could hit targets.

Sometimes we practiced firing at distant targets. For that type of practice, we sent an observer from our squad to a forward position to correct our fire. Since there were no radios, we had to rely on hand signals. It was a very simple system: a hand salute by the spotter to get the attention of the gun commander; a movement of his arms to the left or right to have the gunner adjust his aim from side to side; both arms extended out in front and moved up or down to correct for distance.

Later, in battle, when Spanish comrades had been integrated into our units, these hand signals had to be modified because the Spaniards interpreted them in their own cultural terms, sometimes with tragic consequences. Our signal to "get down" (moving our hands and arms downward) was read by our Spanish comrades as the gesture for "come to me." Because this was such an automatic type of signal for us, it was difficult to remember these differences under the stress and excitement of battle. So we sometimes forgot. More than one Spanish comrade was wounded or killed because of it. The same was true when they called for help by making the same gesture. We would sometimes misinterpret their signal to "come" as "get down" and not support them when they needed us.

Hand signals weren't the only communication problem. There were difficulties with language as well. For instance, I was frequently confused by the word derecha, which translates literally as "right." But if I wanted to say "right" as in "turn right," it was necessary in Spanish to say *mano derecha,* or "right hand." Just saying the single word *derecha* means "straight ahead" or "that's right." At an intersection of roads, if I said *"derecha"* when I wanted the driver to turn right, we'd be in trouble because he would hear the command as "go straight ahead."

Our section leader was Milton Herndon. His position of command was quite a historical event because he and Oliver Law, the commander of the Lincolns, were the first blacks in American history to command white soldiers. Even in World War II, no blacks had such a command. It seemed of such little moment to us that a black was our "boss" that, until doing the research for this book, I had forgotten that Milt was my section commander and that our machine gun company was named the Frederick Douglass Company. Unfortunately, Milt was killed in action soon after we were sent to the front. There weren't many blacks in our battalion, and there were no others in my section, but they were easily accepted without being singled out as special.

That summer, in the center of Spain, I learned how to tolerate the heat and the sun. We would go out in the broiling sun, dig in, and do our practice firing. After experiencing it day after day, I pushed hot weather out of my immediate worries. It was just another part of my new life. I suppose that my natural tolerance for extremes of temperature was enhanced by my reduced body fat, the strengthening of my muscles, and my generally better conditioning. In any case, the heat actually didn't feel harsh. Our American ability to make jokes amid adversity, to laugh at ourselves, certainly helped to get us through the grinding routine. After the struggle of the first couple of weeks, the training program seemed to come easily for me and I did very well. More important, our group learned to work together, to be an organized unit. Learning to work together, to anticipate what our comrades would do, was most necessary when practicing night patrolling and facing the difficulties of trying to fight in darkness.

One of the duties I never could really understand was my periodic assignment to be night duty officer. That meant that, with two other comrades, I patrolled the streets of Tarazona with rifles for which we had no bullets. Every hour or so during our six-hour shift we walked for about fifteen minutes through the village. Then, during the rest of the shift, we sat in the company headquarters and struggled to keep awake. The two with me often napped, but I had to keep awake. All this was ostensibly to make sure that no fascists were trying to infiltrate. It was difficult for me to keep a straight face with my squad, to be soldierly, to take the assignment seriously. I could just see us firing our empty guns at the enemy.

A few times we were marched some five miles to the nearby Jucer River to take a bath. There we stripped to our shorts, splashed and swam and played in a lovely setting in real, although somewhat muddy, water, in a river lined with poplars. For an hour or so we forgot about war. Then we marched back in the heat and dust until we were once again as hot and sweaty as before. But we welcomed these times at the river as real breaks in our routine, which was not only hard but also often boring.

Our Maxims were water-cooled. If they were fired without sufficient coolant, the barrels would overheat and then warp, burst, or at the very least jam. One or more of the crew were assigned the responsibility for having replacement water. Actually, knowing its importance, we all tried to carry extra water. Potable water was limited and rationed, especially at the front. In emergencies, more than once, men urinated into the jacket so they could keep firing.

I learned how to nurse my canteen of water. Instead of pouring water over a toothbrush I dipped the bristles in. Rather than taking a glassful to rinse my mouth, I used only a cautious sip. In place of a bowl of water with which to shave I patted a little on my face and then quickly lathered with a bar of soap. We were admonished, only semi-jokingly, that with one glass of water we should be able to shave, brush our teeth, and have enough left over for a half cup of tea. Without deodorants, full showers, or regular change of clothes, I'm sure that we were always smelly, but as it was universal we soon got used to it and didn't notice.

Marching in the heat was made easier by the singing of some of our Canadian comrades, who came from the south-central provinces of Alberta and Saskatchewan. Of Ukrainian descent, they had a musical ability that set a wonderful rhythm so lilting that we all fell into an easy pattern of marching. Once in a while we would pass German comrades, men from one of the nearby Thaelmann training battalions, who sang German songs. While their singing also seemed to make their marching easier, their songs sounded strident and harsh to my ear and gave the impression of being good only for formal and stiff parading.

My favorite song was one in which many of the lines were improvised. Sometimes we would sing a line in Spanish and then repeat it in English:

Si me quieres escribir	If you wish to write to me
Ya sabes mi paradero	Now you know my address
En el frente de Belchite	In the front of Belchite
Si tu quieres comer bien	If you wish to eat well
Barato y de buena forma	Cheaply and in good style

En el frente de Belchite	In the front of Belchite
Alli hay una fonda	There is an inn
En la entrada de la fonda	In the entrance of the inn
Un Moro, Mojame	There is a Moor, Mojame
Que dice, "Paysa, Paysa	Who says, "Countryman,
Que quieres para comer?"	What do you wish to eat?
El primer plato que se dan	The first course they serve
Son granadas rompedoras	Are grenades that break
El segundo de metralla	And the second shrapnel
Para la memoria	For the memory

Then we would make up lines about the various courses they served, depending upon what the enemy was throwing at us the most—bombs or machine guns or whatever. The name of the front would be changed according to whichever was most active.

After lunch, the second half of the training day frequently started with a meeting held in the village cathedral, which, with the recent separation between the church and the Republic, was no longer used for religious purposes. The topics covered during these assemblies were quite varied. Some were briefings on the progress at the front or on developments in the government, or what was happening on the international scene. Sometimes we had sessions on tactics. Often there were visiting notables, such as novelists Ernest Hemingway or Ralph Bates, both of whom had personal fascination for me because their writings were in some part the inspiration for my coming to Spain. And also because I wanted to emulate them.

Occasionally, an important lecture became ludicrous. I particularly remember one at which a general spoke passionately about commitment and morale and how they would enable us to withstand the enemy's attack, even when things looked their worst. But he spoke in some Slavic language that was then translated into German because the interpreter who knew Slavic wasn't fluent in English. Then it went from German into English via another translator, and after that into Spanish for our Spanish comrades by means of still another. To complicate matters, the translators argued among themselves about the correctness of some of the interpretations. Hearing the speech first in Slavic, then in German, then in English, and finally in Spanish removed all the passion I had sensed in the original. At first it was a fascinating process, and I listened with very focused attention as the general's words went from one language to another. But after a little while my mind began to wander, and I saw that the comrades around me were fidgeting as well. It took more than an hour for his twenty-minute oration to be translated. By the end it had become a comedy of errors, and even the speaker seemed worn down.

But these daily discussions and lectures helped to remind us all of our primary goal. We had come to defeat fascism. In the beginning of our training, the physical demands on our bodies had seemed very heavy, the heat oppressive, the repetition dulling. It was hard for us to remain eager and filled with zeal, and our purpose in being there sometimes got lost from the grind of training, physical exercise more strenuous than most of us were accustomed to, working in weather hotter that we were used to, and submitting to discipline in ways that were foreign. We could easily have lost our focus on saving the nation. These meetings reminded us that we were not just mercenary soldiers but highly motivated ones, who needed more than hardened bodies.

Nothing was greeted with more anticipation than mail call, but it was not an everyday occurrence. It took time for the mail to catch up with us, as troops moved frequently and sometimes we were reassigned to different units. Once in a while the truck carrying the mail broke down, got lost, or was blown up in a bombing raid. In combat positions, mail had an even greater emotional importance than it otherwise would. The more the stress, the more intense our need to maintain a connection with loved ones back home. At the front, the commissar or company clerk handing out the mail would try to catch and hold back all the letters addressed to those who had been killed or wounded. If their names were called, it would remind us all the more of our vulnerability. Nothing was more disappointing than to go to mail call when there wasn't something from home. I saw men who didn't get a letter sneak away and cry.

Because, at first, none of my friends knew where I had gone, and for more than a month after I had left my family were receiving letters from their son that had been posted from New York, I had no initial expectations. But just as soon as I got to Tarazona and had a mailing address to give, I wrote to everyone I knew and asked for letters.

In September, when my first letter telling my parents that I was fighting in Spain arrived home, my father promptly went to the FBI and demanded that they get me back. After all, I was his son! He never wrote to me, but his concern for my safety, his horror at what I was doing, and his hatred for my being on the communist side all came through in letters from my mother, even though there weren't many of those. Her only concerns were my safety and how I could have done this to them.

My friends responded well to my requests for letters. Most of them were fascinated by what I had volunteered to do and honored my decision. Some of my close friends were angry that I hadn't trusted them enough to tell them before I left. A couple even said that, if they had known, they would have come with me.

When the comrade handling the mail didn't call my name, my morale would sink. I, too, felt the ache of disappointment and abandonment, even when my head told me that I shouldn't expect a letter every time. I wrote plenty of letters, something we were encouraged to do as a way of increasing awareness of our struggle back home. Upon my return to UCLA, I found that Lorraine, one of my politically aware friends, had not only saved my letters but had also collected some I'd written to other friends and had arranged to have them printed in the *Daily Bruin*. The paper had featured two full pages of them, one on October 15, 1937, and the other on April 6, 1938.

At the beginning of the war, the armed forces of the Republic were almost completely volunteer militia groups from trade unions and political parties, because almost the entire regular army had defected to the other side. The idea of having officers and ranks was a repugnant one, particularly, although not exclusively, to those units from the anarchist trade unions. The Spaniards had suffered so from the caste system under which they had lived that the whole idea of saluting, saying "sir," or even acknowledging any of the accoutrements of rank was difficult to accept. It took quite a while before anyone wore insignia to indicate officer rank or before anyone saluted, even with the Republican special salute of a clenched fist. Only gradually did the officers stop trying to act like one of the boys.

When given rank, I had the same internal debate. How could we have a democratic, comradely fighting force if officers and men were so separated? But it didn't take too long for me to understand the requirements of command. As officers or noncommissioned officers we had a job to do, which meant our men needed to respond to orders quickly and efficiently.

Now for the first time, I was a leader with some authority. But in this army, authority didn't come automatically with rank. While a marching command of "left" or "halt" was not challenged, in all other instances the men under my command expected me to give reasons for a request or an order. We were young, enthusiastic, and willing, but the idea of being bound by arbitrary rules didn't go down easily.

In some basic sense, we Americans remain civilians in all our wars, always wanting to discuss the whys and wherefores. In Spain, even most of the Communist party members retained this democratic attitude. Consequently, we were always meeting to thrash out problems, to achieve a common understanding, to establish our sense of purpose, and to construct a discipline that seemed fair to us. That did not mean that we were always in opposition to our commanders, just that we felt that this was our army and we should have our say.

In actual combat, of course, there was no time for meetings, no room for discussions of the pros and cons of an action. We either advanced or not, began firing or held our fire, retreated or not, according to command. We did what we were told. But when the action was over, or sometimes even during a lull in the action, we joined in criticism and self-criticism, examining what had happened, how it could have been done better. Often these unofficial, extempory meetings were rancorous—a way to "let off steam" and reduce stress as well as find a better way to do things. With time and experience, a more cohesive spirit emerged that overrode the snafus, the gripes, the boredom, and the defeats of the moment. At the beginning, then, it was self-discipline that brought us together. But we gradually were absorbed by military discipline into a rounded, more compact, responsive organization—but never as automatons.

In the middle of my second month in Spain, I was appointed the political commissar of the machine gun company as an additional, but part-time, assignment. The new assignment, I guessed, was given to me because I was a college student and assumed therefore to be smart, and, because I was a YCLer, presumed to be stable and politically reliable. When given the title I was not sure what it meant, except that the men in my unit translated it into "comic star," a disparaging name conferred on all commissars. At various times commissars were elected by their units or picked by their commanders, but most often they were chosen by the political commissars above them.

There was no school or training courses for me to attend, no classes in my new role. Joe, the battalion commissar, simply told me I had this new and additional duty, that my job was to see that the needs of the men in the company were taken care of as well as was possible, that they were as safe as could be in combat, that they were enthusiastic about their work, that they were in good physical condition, that they were learning to be good soldiers, and that they had the correct political attitude, which, of course, was never defined.

Unlike my part-time assignment, the job of full-time commissar was a rough one, since their working slogan was "First to advance, last to retreat." To be a good commissar meant serving as an example of courage. They had to be tough and straight-talking, being able to gain the confidence of the men while also being tender enough to take care of them. It was something like the job of an ombudsman, but an ombudsman with political and emotional character. The best ones came from the ranks, men who had proved themselves in action. They were to be morale officers and political activists. In combat their function varied, depending on the attitude of the commanding officer, the battle situation, and their own ability. Some commanders shared their command with them, others simply made them into runners. But when a commander was wounded or killed, not infrequently the commissar had to take over command of his unit, at least temporarily.

When away from the front, their job was to look after the quality of the food, to see to recreation, reading material, and health. Equally important, they made sure that the political awareness of the men of their unit was kept high. They had to keep the men current on what was happening in the war beyond the immediate battles and in the outside world. They frequently called meetings just to head off developing problems, to give the men a chance to blow off steam, or sometimes to seek better solutions to problems that arose.

As for me, the only image of the job I had was from the Russian movies I had seen back home, movies in which the commissars were dour, clean-shaven men with powerful chins and broad shoulders, men who made the revolution move forward. All I could figure was that I was to see that the men learned their jobs and worked as a unit. On the democratic side, I was to help solve problems for them by representing them against the higher-ups. Conversely, I would also represent commanders to the men when the men were wrong. But it was another of those jobs without authority.

In World War II, the American army developed a pallid version of the political commissar. Known as orientation officers, their duties seemed most often to be to schedule movies or arrange for athletic events, but they also provided some political propaganda for the troops, including a series of films entitled "Know Why You Fight."

While I was told that one important aspect of my new and extra job was to make sure that the men in my company had the "correct political attitude," I had no real idea of what that political attitude was supposed to be. Hardest of all, I was expected to see that the men were as safe as possible, a responsibility that weighed very heavily. The only way I could figure out how to accomplish that was to try to learn every job in the company, so I would know how best to do them all.

On the first of the month came our first payday. Almost all of us were so naive and idealistic that we were actually surprised when we were paid. When I received my first pesetas I had the slightly nagging thought that I was somehow betraying an ideal, putting a price on what I had come to do. The government, however, paid its soldiers as a cost of government, of running the war, and we were its soldiers. A private wasn't paid much, and the pay, six pesetas a day, wouldn't buy much. It was enough to buy a glass of wine, a cup of coffee, and sometimes a cookie or possibly a piece of cake when we were near a town or village. While we were in Tarazona, we often used this money in the cafes in the evenings when we didn't have night training. Sometimes we bought little extras, such as sweets, which we gave to the village kids. The army carefully observed payday whenever the conditions of war would allow.

Occasionally, we would also get as extras a bar of soap or a pack of cigarettes. These goodies were supplied from home by the Friends of the Abraham Lincoln Brigade, an active support group. Sometimes the extras included an extra issue of toilet paper to supplement what was provided at the toilets. When the European Internationals and the Spaniards saw how much toilet paper the Americans were issued, they were amazed at the quantity. They thought we were pampered and some even called us "politically immature," at least until we had proved ourselves in battle. It didn't seem to me that we were getting so much paper. I was careful, even frugal, with it, but with frequent diarrhea I never had enough.

To call the sanitation in wartime Spain "primitive" is to be polite, and I suspect it was not much better before the war. Bread was often sent to the front uncovered, in open trucks, with an armed soldier sitting on the loaves as a guard. Outside the cities, toilet facilities were often limited and almost always inadequate. In the field, at best there were only trench latrines, most often without disinfectant to control insects or odor—only a pile of loose dirt and a shovel. All of this, combined with the prevalence of flies, the lack of other sanitary practices and facilities, and the absence of enough potable water, made diarrhea and dysentery widespread.

During the seventeen months I spent in Spain, I had either one condition or the other almost a third of the time. On one occasion, I was assigned to go to Madrid with a doctor for supplies, a trip I looked forward to eagerly, for I had never been to the fabled capital city. Unfortunately, I spent the entire two days very close to the toilet in our hotel room.

Medical treatment for dysentery was almost nonexistent. Only a serious bout that included bloody stools and vomiting warranted hospitalization. Once there, bed rest and a bland diet was virtually the only treatment available. Lincoln Battalion surgeon Dr. Bill Pike at one point instituted a program at the front of cleaning dishes with sand, to compensate for the lack of proper dishwashing facilities.

Body and head lice, common to soldiers in most wars, were our constant companions as well. It was commonplace in the barracks, in cafes, and in the trenches to see soldiers with their shirts or pants opened, searching for lice and their eggs, to see buddies combing hair and searching each other's scalps. We became adept at popping lice and eggs between our thumbnails. Some months later I had a wonderful, thick, gray wool scarf that gave me great protection against the winter cold, but I could never permanently rid it of lice. It would have done no good to have thrown it away, because the next one would have quickly become equally infested; the lice were prolific and rapid breeders. Once in a great while a portable shower with hot water and soap would appear. But only when they brought us a deloused change of uniform could we really get clean. Those five-star events were, alas, extremely rare.

I scratched when it was warm and I scratched when it was cold. It seems strange, looking back now, how easily I accepted lice and diarrhea and the lack of sanitation and cleanliness. It wasn't that I liked those conditions, but they didn't depress me very much. I had read the literature of World War I, which was filled with descriptions of the soldiers suffering from lice and grime, and I assumed that they were a natural part of warfare, a price that had to be paid.

CHAPTER
7

Tarazona to Barcelona

In the beginning of September, after almost two months in training, the Mackenzie-Papineau Battalion was a reasonably competent, although untested, military unit. We were ordered out of the arduous but safe habitat of Tarazona. Our initial destination had been to a bivouac in the first of an interminable series of olive groves. As we went from one place to another, it seemed to me that all of Spain was nothing but one huge series of olive groves. Leaving training, we began to have a feeling that we were real soldiers. This new battalion, the Mac-Paps, entered into combat in mid-October at Fuente del Ebro.

One of my most traumatic memories is of the time our battalion was ordered to move from a bivouac in an olive grove to a village some miles away. Recent enemy bombings had been effective in hitting the gasoline storage tanks in our region, so there was no fuel available for the trucks that were to move us. We fell in on the road after an early breakfast. The hopeful rumor was that we were really going to be actually housed, not "olive-groved," at our new destination. Our crew got our machine gun into position on the gravel road so that we could pull it—a task taken jointly by me and the *cabo*, the assistant squad leader.

We marched along the gravel road pulling our guns. As the sun began to rise, it became hot and dusty. While not marching at top, forced-march speed, we did move along fairly quickly. Each full hour of marching was followed by ten minutes of rest, but between these rests I had to drop out along the side of the road periodically because I was suffering from an acute bout of dysentery. What little toilet paper I had scrounged and squirreled away was gone by noon. Then I had to use my few, precious letters from home. That created a dilemma. It was necessary to establish a priority. Maybe I wouldn't have to use them all. Should Lorraine's letter be used first, because I'd be sure to get another from her soon, or should I put that one in last place because if I could keep any letters, hers were the more personal, the most loving? But I used all the letters, and then it was leaves from bushes along the side of the road. After relieving myself, I would have to double-time to catch up, but I was so weak that my legs seemed almost too heavy to move. To this day, I am most penurious with toilet paper.

I could have had other members of the squad take over pulling the gun, but my pride would not let me. They may have been comrades, but I was supposed to be their leader. Not to have done my job would have been the equivalent of quitting, of being unmanly. Toward the end of the day I was stifling tears because it was so hard just to stay upright.

We moved along throughout the morning, had a lunch break, then through the afternoon. Just as it was starting to grow dark, we came to the village. There we were greeted with friendly jeers from the men of other units who had arrived before us and had preempted all the desirable indoor billets. We marched despondently on through the village, making our way to another olive grove a short distance beyond. Bert was there with our rolling kitchen to give us a hot meal, but food didn't interest me by then. In our assigned area, I paid no attention to anything; instead, I scooped out a hip hole in the ground, wrapped myself in my blanket, lay down, and passed out.

Sometime past midnight, I woke from another bowel spasm that came on before I was fully awake, so I soiled my underwear. I stood up groggily, took my shorts off, and cleaned myself with them as best I could. Surrounded by sleeping men on the ground, with no idea of the layout of the camp or the location of the latrine, I walked gingerly in several directions, back and forth, holding my shorts out in front of me, until I finally came to one of the perimeters of the camp. I threw my underwear into the field, then I went back to my hip hole, wrapped myself again in my blanket, and fell instantly asleep.

The agony of that march passed, and my digestive system went back to what had by then become normal, which meant low-level diarrhea rather than intense dysentery. Though we were formally considered combat-ready, our training continued. Our squad's work was good enough so that we were made number one in the company. I automatically became assistant section leader. Because of the greater availability of ammunition, we were now able to do some more practice firing. I began to get the feel for the gun, and I felt that I could fight with it rather than having to fight against it every time I fired.

Everything went well for a while, but as the days went on I continued to lose weight and began to lose energy as well. I could hardly keep up with activities, let alone be a leader. I could not run as fast, as far, nor pull the gun so easily as I had before. Terrified, I wondered if this was because I was afraid of going into combat soon. I doubted myself, castigating myself repeatedly for my lack of courage. This self-flagellation, this sense of shame, gave me enough adrenaline and energy to get through each day—but barely. Each night, however, I would collapse as soon as I could into a sick and miserable sleep, worrying in my dreams about what my comrades thought of my weak behavior, whether I could measure up under fire to the standards for a squad leader I had set for myself.

One day, when we were still just a week or so away from the front and bivouacked in another of Spain's olive groves, the battalion surgeon came by and joined a group of us who were standing, talking about one thing or another. Suddenly I noticed that he was staring at my face.

"What's up?"

"Open your eyes wide," he commanded.

I did, and he looked more intently. "Your eyeballs are yellow."

"So!"

He put his hands on my belly and probed my abdomen. "It's jaundice. You better get your things together. You're going to the hospital now."

"But . . ."

"No buts. We don't play around with jaundice, not with anyone's liver when they have infectious hepatitis, not when a liver is as swollen as yours."

Stunned by the news, I was also elated. In that moment, I fell in love with my jaundiced liver. I would gladly have paraded around the whole camp holding it glistening in my hands to show my comrades. "Look," I wanted to shout, "I'm not a coward. It's not a defect in my head or in my heart; it's just my liver."

I reported the news to Milt, who had the assistant squad leader take over in my place. The battalion ambulance was going for supplies at that moment and would drive past the division hospital, so I was able to get a ride with the driver. It seemed an endless trip, even sitting in the relatively comfortable front seat. At the hospital admitting room, it didn't take the examining doctor long to confirm the battalion surgeon's diagnosis. There were no lab tests made, no X-rays taken; all they did was look at my eyes and feel my abdomen. The doctor admitted me into the hospital and said that I would not be able to return to my unit for at least a couple of months, possibly longer, for the only treatment available for this condition was rest and a bland diet. I was flooded with a real stew of emotions—relief that I was really sick, guilt at being taken out of action just as we were on the brink of combat, and shock and dismay at the idea of having nothing to do for several months.

As my disease was not considered contagious if reasonable sanitary precautions were taken, I pleaded with the doctor to let me do something useful around the hospital. I told him that I had a background in bacteriology and laboratory work, that at Los Angeles City College I had worked in the Bacteriology Department as a teaching assistant, and that at UCLA one of the jobs I had had was working in the Zoology Department's experimental laboratory. As a premedical student, I had taken all sorts of science courses. Also, for a couple of years I had worked as a research assistant for a doctor in private practice, helping him with his work on the treatment of arthritis. I knew I had some skills that could be useful, and I couldn't bear the idea of doing nothing for months.

The doctor heard me out but made no promises. Then, about an hour or so later, he came to my bed and handed me a thousand *pesetas* and a *Salvo Conducto* (pass and authorization to travel) to Barcelona. "Go to Barcelona," he said, "and buy the equipment necessary to set up a small clinical laboratory."

To say that I was stunned was the understatement of the war. Even though I had worked in labs, I had never set one up. How would I do it? What would I need? Where would I go in Barcelona? Did I have enough money?

To all my protestations the doctor replied, "You can do it! We need the lab. Our medical supply can't seem to come up with what we need. We want the standard urine and blood tests, such as for albumen and sedimentation rates, at the very least a Gram staining procedure so we know what's in infected wounds, simple things like that. We don't have to make bacterial cultures, although that would, of course, be wonderful."

"But, but, I don't know all the things that are necessary. I'm not sure I'll know what to buy or where to get them."

I felt lost, as if I had oversold myself. But to all my disclaimers he just answered, "You can do it! Go to Barcelona! I know you don't feel good, but people don't die from jaundice, and you'll get some rest in Barcelona. The change will do you good."

I didn't speak more than a few words of Spanish. I was sick and running a 103-degree fever. I was weak and had lost thirty-five pounds. I barely knew where Barcelona was, and I certainly knew nothing about setting up a laboratory.

But to all my misgivings the doctor simply replied, "You can do it! I know you can."

I sat, excited and frightened, on my cot. On the adjoining cot was an ambulance driver who knew Barcelona. He suggested that I go to the headquarters of the British Medical Aid Service, which provided rooms for their personnel and drivers who passed through.

"Lynette, who's in charge there is a fine person. She'll help you, I'm sure. She gave me a bunk for a couple of days."

I finally got my courage together and left the hospital. I hitched a ride to the nearest railhead, some forty miles away, getting a ride on the back of an open truck. I sat on its empty steel bed, bracing myself against the back of the cab, suffering from the wind, shivering from fever. The driver let me out at the railroad station, where I collapsed on the floor, leaning back against a wall, waiting for the train to Barcelona. When I'd finally boarded, I found that sitting upright on the coach's wooden seats required more strength and energy than I had. I lay down on the dirty floor under the seat, behind the legs of the other passengers, put my small sack of clothes and toiletries under my head, and slept. Toward the end of the trip, I was able to sit up on the bench.

I have no idea of how long it took, how many stops we made. A very caring Jewish couple, Pedro and Jonna Steffan, who lived in Barcelona, helped me. With a little Spanish and a little Yiddish, they comforted me when I awakened and shared their food, although I wasn't very hungry. Unfortunately, I knew no more Yiddish than I did Spanish, for my parents had been on a complete assimilation course. They had used Yiddish only when they didn't want me to understand what they were saying. Even that little bit of Yiddish conversation had stopped the first time my newly acquired high school German allowed me to penetrate their code.

My instructions had been, "Go to Barcelona and buy equipment." They did not include how or where. When the train lurched to a stop in the station, I stood up and must have looked lost and bewildered, which I was. The Steffans took me, one on each arm, and led me up onto the street and to a bus stop. Somehow, they managed to carry their packages, too. When the right bus came along, they put me on it. Jonna kissed me on the cheek and Pedro patted my shoulder and said, *"Adios."* He then turned to the driver, paid my fare, and at some length instructed him how to take care of me.

After not too long a ride, the driver stopped the bus and began to talk to me, telling me where to go. When my blank face showed I wasn't understanding, he pointed in the direction I was to walk. Then, with the map my friends from the train had drawn, I started off. The British Service was within a block of where I had been let off the bus.

It was a large, marble-fronted apartment building that before the war had been inhabited by very well-to-do people. In the foyer, pasted over the list of former apartment owners, was a hand-lettered list of tenants, all new to the building. A small wire-cage elevator took me up the five floors, and there, directly in front of the elevator, was a cardboard sign for the Medical Service. I rang the bell, and Lynette, who was in charge of the Barcelona station, opened the door.

"Yikes," she cried, seeing that I was about to pass out.

She guided me down the hall and put me into a bed. Not only did she give me room and board for the week that I stayed in the city, but she also fed me far, far better than I had been accustomed to in the past months. We had fresh vegetables, some fruits, and even some meat. After a couple of days I began to recover some strength, and by midweek my temperature had dropped, if not to normal, then at least close to it.

Except during that arrival weekend, when I slept for almost two days and nights, I spent each day going from one medical supply house to another in search of equipment. I would slowly walk east, down from the apartment building, cross the main plaza, then go down the gently sloping ten blocks or so of the Ramblas de las Flores to the waterfront, where most of the medical supply houses were located. Fortunately, there were benches on the Ramblas, so I could stop every block or so and rest, making it possible for me to make the trek even in my weakened condition. The Ramblas was also the street on which the prostitutes worked, and I watched them and their johns as I rested on the benches. My interest was only intellectual, for my libido at that time was practically gone.

For the first couple of days I barely made it, collapsing on my bed for a couple of hours each time I got back to the apartment. I went out every day with a tiny English-Spanish dictionary and a list of the equipment and tests I thought I needed, and each afternoon I came back carrying some piece of equipment in a bag, a small part of my task fulfilled. Negotiations were often prolonged and difficult because of my limited knowledge of some of the apparatus. In labs at school, equipment had been provided and I'd used it, but I knew little about its installation or limitations. There were also instruments that I had used but didn't know the names of, which made looking for them a real problem. And some of the standard reagents went by names different from those to which I was accustomed. Sometimes I had to search, because the Spanish used different reagents or supplies than I was used to. Sometimes they were out of the specific item I wanted, and then we had to rummage for substitutes. Every house had sizable gaps in its inventory. Each item sought required drawing, pantomime, and gyrations on my part, along with the inevitable searches in my little dictionary.

Our efforts to understand one another were sometimes ludicrous, sometimes maddening. I even tried my high school German, which some of the people I dealt with knew better than English. But then they would speak quickly in a more complex and fluent German than I was capable of handling. So I'd be lost again.

To further complicate my attempts, I knew only the familiar tu instead of the formal usted form of speech. The informal/familiar mode of speech was obligatory in the International Brigades and in most of the Republic as a symbol of democracy. The formal speech represented class divisions that were no longer acceptable. Prior to the Republic, addressing someone in the familiar form (except for children, servants, members of the family, or very close friends) had implied that the person was an inferior, someone of a lower class or status. And formal usage was an important sign of respect for older persons.

This class division was one of the things that the Republic was trying to eliminate, but these commercial gentlemen had used the formal usted all their lives. They were kind enough to tolerate both my ignorance of the language and my ineptitude, and did not take my familiarity as a discourtesy. They were polite and eager to support the war effort.

Finally, toward the end of the week, I found one salesman who was reasonably fluent in English. He filled in the gaps for me, writing lists in Spanish or Catalan, and sent me to those places he thought most likely to have what I needed. In some cases, it meant backtracking to shops where I had been unsuccessful earlier. With the help of his lists, I finally got most of what I needed to take blood samples, do bacteriological stains, and perform many of the necessary chemical tests.

During my trips back and forth, I came to realize that I was claustrophobic about being underground during a bombing or the threat of one. Several times, when I'd been crossing the Plaza de Catalyuna, the main square of the city, the sirens had announced that enemy planes were on their way from the fascist-held Balearic Islands off to the east. Everyone in the immediate area was forced to go down into the metro station at the plaza, but I hated it. I wasn't trying to be macho or show bravery. It was simply that being in a shallow trench was less stressful to me than being in an underground bunker. If I could spot the planes, I could track them visually and compute in my head the point they would have to reach for their bombs not to hurt me. Most of all, in a trench I wasn't afraid of being buried alive. Fifty years later, in my hot tub high in the Berkeley hills, I would find myself automatically doing the same sort of tracking and computing while watching a plane take off from the San Francisco airport and head my way, still tensing for a moment until I could adjust to where I was, or perhaps better, to where I wasn't.

Barcelona had remnants of peacetime activity in its food stores, cafes, and nightclubs, but the evidence of war was everywhere: destruction from bombing, the presence of troops, street barricades. Banners calling for the defeat of fascism, for victory, and supporting increased productivity in the factories were strung across the narrow streets, particularly in the working-class neighborhoods. Posters and leaflets were nailed to trees and fastened to lampposts. "Is there an able-bodied man in your factory?—Why isn't he at the front?" they shouted. "To defend Madrid is to defend Catalonia," they exhorted.

On the last night of my stay, Lynette had a date with a Catalonian intelligence officer. For some reason, she invited me to go along. Alfonso turned out to be a dapper, slightly built man, about five-feet-eight with a carefully trimmed mustache, an immaculate, perfectly tailored uniform, and the most beautiful, brightly polished boots I had ever seen. He wasn't overly pleased with my intrusion on his date, but he took it gracefully in stride. We walked to a nightclub a few blocks away. Because I couldn't understand what the performers were saying, and because I didn't want to intrude into the date any more than I already had, I went to the back of the club and sat at the bar with my back to the stage, sipping beer.

There I enjoyed this slice of semicivilian life and watched the performance on the stage in the mirror at the back of the bar. It was a bit like watching television with the words blanked out but the sound still on. A guitarist provided background music for the two or three performers, who sang, danced, and performed a comedy routine. Watching the performers in the mirror react to each other, seeing them not in military formation, not giving or obeying orders except in parody, and hearing the laughter of the audience was a lovely change. I could see Alfonso and Lynette talking to each other, laughing, drinking, touching each other. *"Un otra cerveza, por favor"*—Another beer, please, was about all that I could say. But it was enough to make for a memorable and relaxing evening.

Afterward, we walked back to the apartment in the dark, Alfonso and Lynette arm in arm. As protection against air raids, the few streetlights were shaded so that they gave little light, none visible from the sky. At night electric power was rationed mainly to factories and to a few businesses such as restaurants or the club we had come from. None went to dwellings. Nevertheless, the streets were teeming, as Spanish cities always seem to be at night.

Entering our apartment building, I started to say good night with the idea of letting them end the evening as they would. Suddenly, Lynette gave a delicate burp, a little gasp, and passed out, gently, even gracefully, collapsing onto the marble floor. She'd been hit by the alcohol she had been drinking, much too liberally, at the cafe.

Startled, the captain looked at her with a stony face, looked up the wide, open stairwell toward the apartment on the fifth floor, looked down at her, looked at me. He repeated this several times. Then he clicked the heels of his beautifully polished boots together, saluted me precisely and properly with clenched fist, made the suggestion of a bow, murmured *"buenos noches"*—all in one graceful, flowing motion—then made a perfect, regulation about-face and marched out into the night.

Bewildered, I also looked up that stairwell that stretched five double floors to our apartment. At night there was no electricity to run the elevator. I thought guiltily of leaving her to sleep it off. But obligation and my sense of chivalry caught up with me. I hefted Lynette onto my shoulder, fireman's carry, and slowly started up the stairs, half pulling myself up on the banister. After reaching the first floor, I had to rest quite a while. By the second floor I was crawling on my hands and knees, with her still on my back. I'll never know how I made it up the last three flights.

Inside the apartment, I crawled with her on my back to her bedroom and, with my last ounce of energy, tossed her off my shoulder onto her bed. Then I collapsed on the floor alongside and passed out. At some point, while it was still dark outside, she woke me and invited me into her bed. But much as I would have liked to, I didn't have the energy to get up from the floor, let alone perform for her sexual pleasure, or mine. She cursed me roundly, using some British swear words I had never heard before. Agonized, I crawled down the hall to my bedroom, where next to my bed I collapsed again, also on the floor.

Sometime during the night, I woke and summoned enough energy to get into bed. Later in the morning, I finally gathered myself together, got washed, bundled up my acquisitions, thanked Lynette as if nothing untoward had happened the night before, and left for the front with my two big bags full of laboratory goodies and a tiny bag with some fruit and cheese.

CHAPTER
8

Grañen

When I had left on this trip to Barcelona, the hospital was already under orders to move north and west to the Huesca front. From the doctor at the hospital, in addition to the *pesetas* and *salvo conducto*, I had received a hand-drawn map showing the route through the villages that would take me to the new location of the hospital. Having said good-bye to Lynette, I went to the corner across from the apartment building and took a bus to the outskirts of town. There were enough army trucks going in the right direction whose drivers were lonely and eager for company, so hitching was not difficult. My two large cloth bags were not a problem, even though they were so big and heavy I could barely carry them.

While getting a ride was easy, communication was not. I knew the word *donde*, which meant "where," so if they asked I could show my map and point to the villages I had to go through. And I could answer when they pointed to me and asked, *"Donde?"* I could reply *"Soy Americano"* (I am an American) and *"Voy a Grañen"* (going to Grañen), but after that it was difficult.

A couple of the drivers kept talking to me even though I made it clear to them that I couldn't understand most of what they were saying. The drivers were so lonely and bored that they talked to any warm body. Apparently conversing is what they did when they had company, and for them I was company. The long hours alone in vehicles that often were barely roadworthy, along roads that were frequently clogged with slow-moving traffic and torn up from bombings or lack of upkeep, made driving extremely hard work. So it was no surprise that they appreciated the company, even of someone as mute as me. Two offered to share their meager lunch with me, a sandwich or some bread. I, in turn, gave them some of the fruit I had been able to buy in one of the small stores near the Barcelona apartment.

On my fourth and last hitch to the Huesca region above Zaragoza, only a few kilometers before my destination, the truck crested a hill and there, lying before us, was the broad valley in which Grañen was located. Suddenly we heard the explosion of bombs and the firing of machine guns from planes. The driver immediately pulled over to the side of the road, jammed on his brakes, and killed the motor. We both jumped out, dashed off the road, ran to distance ourselves in case a plane opened fire on the truck, and threw ourselves down into the ditch that ran alongside the road. After a few minutes, we raised our heads and peeked out to see whether it was an enemy plane or one of ours. We had learned to head for shelter every time an explosion sounded, and only afterward to try to determine whose planes were overhead and whether they signaled immediate danger. The sound of any plane was a notice to be on guard, since there were so few on the government's side. To add to the uncertainty, once in a while our side fought with captured equipment, and the fascists often camouflaged theirs with red bands on the wings, the Republic's insignia.

An aerial attack in this sector was completely unexpected and startling, as there had been virtually no fighting in this area for months. Until a short time ago, our troops here had been composed of volunteers from the anarchist trade unions, and the atmosphere had been so peaceful, so unwarlike, that an arrangement had been made with the fascists for a daily truce so that the two sides could play soccer in no-man's-land.

On the plain ahead, about a mile from us, eight to ten planes flew in a circle over a small pueblo. In a sort of merry-go-round formation, each would dip down, drop a small bomb, fire a brief burst from its guns, and then rise up again into the circular pattern from which it had come. Then the next plane in the formation followed. When each of them had done its part in the attack, the aerial pack flew to an adjoining pueblo and repeated the maneuver. When they ran out of bombs, they repeated these attacks using only their machine guns. It was almost as if they were going from house to house doing Halloween pranks. After they had finished terrorizing the countryside, they turned tail and went back home in regular V formation. In later years, we realized that the German planes and pilots had been perfecting the blitzkrieg, the terror attack that they would use with such devastating effect in World War II.

Even though I could see that the planes were almost a mile away and heading generally away from us, my body became rigid, the tenseness of fear that came whenever their planes were bombing or strafing in the immediate vicinity. It was almost as if my autonomic nervous system could not believe what my brain was processing about their distance from us.

When the planes had disappeared into the distance, we got back in the truck and started off again. Soon I was let off in the small main plaza of the little village of Grañen with my two sacks of prized laboratory equipment. Grañen was a poor, sleepy little agricultural town whose most important structures were the church and the home of the rich landowner. Since both the clergy and the landlord had fled at the start of the war, the church was being used as a school, and our hospital was located in the landowner's home, which was just at the edge of town. Originally, the hospital had been in a dilapidated farmhouse, but now it was in an elegant and relatively grandiose structure standing in stark contrast to the rest of the small village. The interior was typical of the way the rich in the small villages had displayed their wealth—mosaic tile on the floor, richly paneled walls, stained-glass windows. The huge two-storied kitchen with a big wood-burning stove was at the back, dwarfing the rest of the rooms. Curiously, although the rest of the house had been stripped bare before our arrival, there were still several oil paintings hanging on the walls.

Even with the size of this house and the large number of rooms, most of the space was reserved for patients, so that the cots of the hospital personnel, including medical officers, were jammed into small upstairs rooms. Because the sector was so quiet, there was no rush of patients. We couldn't understand why our hospital had been relocated here, except to speculate that there must have been a planned offensive that was later canceled. Most of the patients were being treated for illness, and the surgery was used to treat accident patients.

I was given a small room on the ground floor, hardly bigger than a large closet but with enough light from a single small window to keep it from being too dark or drab. Outside my window was a grove of trees, some olive, others lemon. This was to be the lab as well as my sleeping quarters. My cot was crowded back into one end of the room. Boards on top of a couple of wooden boxes made my desk and lab table. My storage space was inside the boxes holding up my desk. I carried water into the lab in a five-gallon glass carboy and the waste out in a slop bucket. Despite my Barcelona acquisitions and what I had been able to scrounge from the hospital, my lab was primitive and limited. I had been able to acquire much of the necessary equipment, but I didn't have all of the reagents I needed. What I'd brought from Barcelona wasn't nearly enough; a thousand pesetas didn't go far, even with price controls.

The first test I was called upon to perform was the examination of a urine sample for albumin, the presence of which would indicate that the patient's kidneys or urinary system was in trouble. The test is relatively simple. The urine is heated in a test tube. If it shows a cloudiness, that can be either phosphates, which don't indicate bodily malfunction, or albumin, which could signal danger. The determination between the two is made by adding a little weak acid to the heated solution, which causes the phosphates to dissolve. Albumin, if present, remains as a cloud. Because I didn't have butane gas for my Bunsen burner, I couldn't heat the test tube in the lab. I carefully took the filled test tube down to the kitchen and asked the chef's permission to use the stove.

"Get out of here," he yelled at me, "and don't come back until lunch is finished. I don't want you to louse up my food with the stink of piss. And be sure you aren't here late so you don't fuck up my dinner prep."

Right after lunch I brought my sample back again, heated it carefully over the stove, and cloudiness appeared. "Can I have a little vinegar please? It's all I need to finish the test."

"No," he roared. "I have too little to waste on your craziness."

After fuming for a few minutes at his unwillingness to help me, I went out into the orchard in back of the hospital, picked a green lemon from a tree, and squeezed a little juice into the sample. The citric acid from the lemon did the job. The cloud dissolved. The doctor could stop worrying about albumin in making his diagnosis.

The days went by, and my work kept me fairly busy. Talking with the doctors, I kept learning more about the clinical aspects of lab work, and I began to develop some self-confidence. I learned to take blood samples for tests, either by pricking a finger or by putting a needle and syringe into a vein. I had performed these functions only a few times back home, so few that I had to learn the skills all over again.

My health began to improve. Daily inspection in a mirror showed the yellow disappearing from my eyes. One of the doctors taught me how to feel my liver, and each day my fingers pressed into my belly. As time went by, my liver was subsiding to somewhere close to normal size. I even put back a couple of pounds of my lost weight. About once a week one of the staff doctors would examine me. My appetite was good and most of my energy had returned, and so I began to think about returning to the front. When I asked the doctors when I could leave, however, their answers were noncommittal or "not yet."

From time to time, news would come about the Mac-Paps—where they were stationed, what action they were in, which of my comrades had been wounded or killed. I wondered whether my position as head of a machine gun squad would still be open for me. One day, after a little more than a month, to my utter surprise, papers came through officially transferring me out of my machine gun company, out of the Mackenzie-Papineau Battalion, and assigning me permanently to the Servicio Sanitario (Medical Service) of the 35th Division, to which our hospital was attached. I finished my year and a half of service in the hospitals of the 35th. I had not made application for this change, had not even considered that my work here was other than temporary.

Not only was life physically much easier as a medic than as a machine gunner, but the new orders must also surely have saved my life, as the Brigaders were always assigned to the most active battlefront. The mortality rate for Americans was at least 30 percent overall, and of the survivors, almost 80 percent were wounded, many more than once. If noncombatant volunteers, such as ambulance drivers, administrators, and medical personnel, were deducted from this computation, the percentage of our casualties at the front skyrocketed. The odds for survival were even lower for machine gunners, who were always prime targets. And heads of gun crews had the lowest survival rate of all.

Looking back, I can't regret my transfer, since the odds for my surviving on the front were pretty slim. But at that time I had many qualms, feeling that I was not doing my share, that this was not what I had volunteered to do. So I argued with myself, wondering whether to demand a return to my unit, whether the job I was doing was important enough to justify being out of combat. All the time I was there I never quite put away the tremor of guilt that I wasn't doing enough, the feeling that I wasn't doing my share of the good fight. I broached the idea of my return to combat several times, but the doctors I was working with laughed at the idea or just turned down my request, saying that they needed me where I was, that they had work for me to do that would help the functioning of the hospital.

In some ways, I suppose, I appreciated the relative safety of working in the hospitals, which, while close to the front and frequently bombed and strafed, were different from being in the direct line of enemy fire. And yet, while being bombed is never a pleasure, in the trenches, where danger is perpetual, having a weapon in your hands permits the illusion of not being totally helpless.

I remember a time in the Grañen hospital when I was about to take a blood sample from a patient. Without the usual warning of the rapid ringing of church bells, the walls shook and our ears hurt from the explosions of a surprise aerial bombardment. My mouth suddenly had that same horrible, metallic taste that comes when tinfoil is placed against a tooth with a silver filling. That intense fear came over me at moments when the unexpected happened and I didn't have time to prepare myself. I dropped to the floor and rolled under a table to protect myself against shrapnel or falling beams, all the while holding my sterile syringe in the air so that it wouldn't be contaminated.

Although the numbing, paralyzing fright abated after a few moments, my heart kept pounding away. One of the orderlies was on the floor with a sack of bread over him, another was under a bed with the patient still in it. Just ahead of me, one of the doctors, a German, was on his haunches, balancing with one hand on a cot. I don't know whether he was trying to project a sense of calmness or whether he was just frozen with fear. At the entrance to the room, a nurse had rolled against one of the walls. Another nurse was beside a bed, trying to calm a patient who was thrashing about.

Then, after what seemed hours but was actually only a few minutes, the bombing came to an end. While no all-clear signal was given, the sound of the planes faded into the distance and we began to tend to the patients. One was halfway under his mattress and trying weakly to get farther underneath; another was flailing about in spite of the nurse who was trying to keep him from harming himself; a couple of patients were on the floor. All had to be quieted and comforted. In the surgical ward, some had to be treated for wounds that had reopened after their panicked attempts to get to safety.

One of the unit's doctors happened to be in the next pueblo, about two kilometers away, at the time of the attack. Seeing the fumes and smoke from the bombing, he thought that all of our pueblo and the hospital must have been wiped out. When the attack was over, he rushed back to find that there was only one house destroyed by a direct hit. All that was left of it was a partial shell of three walls and, in the middle, a smoking mass of burning wood. Four or five other homes had been partially damaged in such a way that they could be repaired without a great deal of effort. A couple of the streets had large holes from bomb explosions that would have to be filled and resurfaced. Our hospital suffered a couple of holes in the roof from gunfire, and one of the nurses had a blouse hanging on her bedroom wall that was torn by a bullet. A few civilians had been wounded, and they were brought to us for treatment.

Children of the region, in fact all over the Republic, were taught to play next to their neighborhood *refugio,* into which they rushed whenever the church bell or siren gave the air-raid alarm. This time, fortunately, even without advance warning, the kids had reacted quickly enough. The *refugios* in Grañen were not underground shelters, only narrow, sand-bagged trenches. One of the worst sights of the war was seeing these kids huddled together, jammed close as if to find their safety in one another, the younger ones often whimpering in their fear, the older ones tight-lipped, trying to hold back their tears, trying to comfort the younger. I often wondered how those kids could come out of that experience even close to psychologically whole.

Once, when I had to go back to the division infirmary from one of our advance hospitals, I hitched a ride in a small evacuation ambulance. It had racks for four stretchers. One of the evacuees was from the Mac-Paps machine gun company, though not from my squad, and so I rode with him in back, instead of up front with the driver. Alex had lost so much of his left forearm from artillery shrapnel that it had been amputated above the elbow. I stood next to his stretcher, having to stoop just a little because the ceiling was low.

Just after the driver closed the back doors on us and started the engine, planes arrived overhead and began to strafe and bomb us. We could hear them whine down toward us with their guns open. The whistle of those bullets is a sound that is etched in my memory. My throat closed, my chest heaved, as the fear hit. I couldn't move to get out of the ambulance because I didn't want to leave Alex, so I kept telling myself, "If you jump out, you'll probably go straight into the path of a bullet." But the rationalization didn't stop my fright. I stood there holding Alex's good hand and raging at the fascists for being uncivilized barbarians, for attacking medical units and ambulances.

As soon as he could get the engine going, the driver drove as fast as he could, zigzagging down the road. Since the ambulance was only a converted truck with stiff springs, and the road was badly rutted, the stretchers bounced and swayed back and forth violently as he made his turns from one side to the other. When we were out of range of the planes, the driver slowed down to normal speed and drove in a straight line. But even then the vehicle was such an old cheesebox that the stretchers leaped about and made the trip an agonizing, screaming hell for my friend. With the worst of the shaking he would cry out, almost in a whimper, "Oh mother! Oh mother!" I kept wishing that the pain would knock him out, but it didn't.

I put my woolen cap under his head, which helped a little, for it kept the back of his head from hitting the iron rack. But his raw stump kept banging against the canvas, so I put my left hand under his shoulder, bracing my wrist against the round metal bar that held the stretcher, hoping that I could minimize the bouncing. My right hand grasped his good hand, but the whole of my hand seemed too much for him to hold, so he just grabbed my thumb and he never let go during the entire long trip. I kept talking throughout the gruesome ride, partly to distract him but also in an attempt to maintain control of myself. I don't know what I said, what I talked about, I just kept talking.

The drive never seemed to end. We had to cross a small mountain range where, at the top, it became bitterly cold. Each of the wounded men had only a single blanket. When we finally got to the hospital, my hand was bloody and my wrist bruised from bracing myself against the iron railing. My thumb was sore from his tight grasp, and my throat rasped both from talking so much and from the contractions that came from fear.

On the other side of the ambulance, in the upper stretcher, a Spanish soldier had started to cough blood during the trip. I had nothing to give him. He died en route. The two lower stretcher cases had fortunately passed out, either from anesthetic or from shock. They both survived the trip, as did Alex, who, when he recovered, was sent back home.

Some months later word came to me through one of the ambulance drivers that my Bulgarian friend, Eric, whom I had met in Figueras, had been killed almost immediately upon going to the front with the Dimitrov (Slavic) Battalion of the 13th Brigade. We had been together on the train from Figueras to Albacete, but after they had split us up by language, I had not seen or heard from him again.

By the time the news came to me, death and the maiming of comrades had become an agonizing daily reality. I dealt with the injured daily and watched many of them die. While I mourned for Eric, I clamped down on the grief, fearful that otherwise it would devour me. I felt sorrow but no regret. Regret would have meant denying the righteousness of our cause, relinquishing the justification for putting our lives at risk. Regret would have meant thinking that we shouldn't have come. That did not mean that I was immune to sadness, only that I managed, on the one hand, to let it hit me only in little bits at a time, and, on the other, to look at it dispassionately, much as a surgeon must do when tending to a wounded body. It was a confused, conflicting pattern of fears, feelings, and denial, but I had no other way to cope with the horror. As I became more and more integrated in the medical service, my focus became saving the wounded, not killing the enemy.

The front lines were sometimes so fluid, often on such steep and treacherous hillsides and so frequently exposed to enemy gunfire, that the stretcher-bearers had to carry the wounded for a half-hour or even longer to get them out of the line of fire and to an aid station. The casualty rate for bearers was high, their exhaustion rate even higher. At times, almost anyone could and would be required to help with bearer service. Even officers going back to their headquarters for a briefing might be pressed into duty. Where possible, ambulances were brought up very close to the front, but that was often difficult and dangerous. While the table of organization assigned at least one ambulance per battalion, often that turned out to be only a paper assignment, for the ambulance never arrived. Or if it was attached, it might not be functional, undergoing repairs. Unfortunately, neither the ambulances nor hospitals with their red crosses were immune from attack. Often we felt that hospitals were choice targets of the Nazi pilots. Only those few base hospitals that were beyond bombing range had red crosses visible on their roofs. Otherwise, ambulances and hospitals were camouflaged as much as possible.

One of the contributions our army introduced to war medicine was having its primary hospitals close to the front lines. In the fighting in Madrid, our medical people saw the need for quick care. There, the battle lines were often within walking distance of the hospitals. This meant that only minimal and the most urgent treatment was given at the aid stations—tourniquets, bandages, surface cleaning of wounds, immobilizing of broken bones so that they wouldn't shatter further during transport. At most, and then only very occasionally, a few emergency stitches. This close-up hospitalization made serious, life-saving treatment more quickly available.

The stories of medical evacuation in the first days of the war (except in Madrid, where patients had to be moved only yards, not miles) were nothing short of horrendous. There was a shortage of doctors and trained nurses, and those who were available were assigned to the established hospitals in the rear. Convention had it that it was there that their skills could be put to best use. What were called forward hospitals in the first few months were nothing more than collecting stations where the wounded were accumulated until there were enough to justify sending a trainload back to a real hospital. They rarely had surgical facilities, sometimes no doctors, often no trained nurses. The only treatment might be a shot of morphine to ease the pain.

So the concept was born of front-line hospitals in order to shorten the time from the wounding to the repairing. To accomplish this goal, these surgical units had to be capable of following advances and, if necessary, in the case of retreats, of pulling up stakes quickly. This meant that no elaborate construction was done to house these forward locations. We used what was available, and that was quite varied: churches, homes, railway tunnels, caves, convents, tents. In turn, this mobile approach meant that the wounded at these forward installations were not kept any longer than absolutely necessary after treatment.

The overall organization of the military, added to the entrance of Internationals, brought in enough doctors, nurses, and ambulance drivers to start filling the void. As the war went on, a patterned medical service was established. Patients were brought to our advance hospitals, close to the front. There they were operated upon. Then, as soon as they were in stable enough condition, they were evacuated to the nearest base hospital with open bed space. In these more secure and stable installations in the rear, there were facilities for recuperation, physical therapy, and more complicated reconstructive surgery. The surgery and treatment at the advance hospitals, where I was stationed most of the time, emphasized more immediate life-saving procedures.

Wounds were cleaned and drains installed. This was the time before sulfa drugs or antibiotics, which not only meant slower recovery but also often required that wounds not be closed. The flesh had to be allowed to drain, which meant keeping the wound open. Broken bones were set and limbs put in plaster casts that allowed for drainage of the suppurating wound. Dr. Tueda was the inventor of this plaster treatment. In the case of a compound fracture, even with an infected wound, he would put the entire area in plaster and leave it there for days or even weeks. When the plaster was taken off, the wound and the fracture were often healed.

Abdominal and chest operations removed bullets or shrapnel and sewed up torn tissues. Shattered bones were given minimal treatment, the limb immobilized so the soldier could be transported back without doing further damage. Surgery was justified only when not performing it would put the wounded's life in peril or lessen his chances for full recovery, such as in the case of bone fragments driven into musculature or a torn blood vessel. The pressure from the accumulation of patients waiting for treatment often was the critical factor in deciding what medical or surgical procedures would be undertaken, although occasionally an exception might be made if a particular wound was surgically interesting or challenging to the doctor. This mobile, advanced pattern of treatment made the ability to move the wounded promptly—both from the battlefield by stretcher and then by ambulance to the hospital—critically important. From there back to base installations, movement was by ambulance or train.

In November of 1936, Dr. Norman Bethune, a thoracic surgeon from Canada, arrived in Madrid. He visited the front lines, which were often not much more than a hundred yards away from streetcar stops. He inspected casualty stations and then the base hospitals. He studied the types of wounds. Then, at the city hospitals to which the men were taken, he analyzed recovery rates. After traveling from Madrid to Albacete, inspecting hospitals and medical facilities, he had an interview with one of the chief medical officers of the International Brigades, Dr. Erwin Kisch, a Czech volunteer.

Bethune pointed out that it was feasible to provide transfusions at forward aid stations, even very close to the battlefields. He therefore proposed the establishment of mobile transfusion units, which would gather donations of blood from volunteers in the cities and transport the collected blood as close to the fighting as possible. In arguing for the establishment of this system, he admitted that never in all modern warfare, even with the most highly organized medical services, had it been done.

With Kisch's agreement he went to Valencia, where he got approval from Soccoro Rojo (Red Aid) headquarters, the trade union relief group that during the first half-year of the war was the only effective medical service in the country. The government Sanidad Militar (military medical organization) took over in the spring of 1937. Then Bethune telegraphed back to Canada to the Spanish Aid Committee in Toronto for funds and immediately set out for Paris and London. When he reached Paris, he found that ten thousand dollars had been cabled to him. With this money he bought sterilizers, instrument sets, and other apparatus for this project. Packing some 1,875 pieces of surgical equipment, collecting flasks, hurricane lamps, and the like into a Ford station wagon, Bethune started south.

When he reached the Spanish border, he was enraged when the French government demanded a large exit fee.

Blood transfusions were first performed by a doctor in Rome in 1492, but it wasn't until 1613 that William Harvey discovered the circulation of blood. The use of blood in treating the sick and wounded passed in and out of favor for centuries because, not knowing about blood types, sterile techniques, and other causes of negative reactions, doctors were not often successful in using the new treatment. Most of the early transfusions resulted in anaphylactic shock, massive infection, and often death.

One of the problems with the storage of blood was that it quickly clotted and became useless. That obstacle was overcome when in 1915 Dr. Richard Lewisohn in the United States and Professor L. Agote in Buenos Aires independently found that adding sterile sodium citrate to blood harmlessly prevents coagulation. A decade later, Russian doctors discovered that refrigerated, citrated blood could be stored for six weeks and still be useful for transfusions. Not long afterward, a simple understanding of blood types was achieved and systemized. It was found that people with one type, who were called universal donors, were able to donate to almost any recipients without causing adverse reactions. It was from this group that the reserves were to be built. At the beginning of the war, Dr. Duran Jorda of Barcelona had done some excellent practical work on ways of storing blood and organizing blood banks. Later, he was appointed chief of the nation's Blood Transfusion Service, and I was fortunate to have worked under him, if only briefly.

On December 6, Bethune returned to Madrid with his instruments and equipment, gathered a crew, and began to set up a laboratory/clinic in an eleven-room apartment that had been taken from the German embassy's legal counsel. A few volunteers, including Bethune himself, typed their blood samples and took medical histories to make sure that they were not carrying malaria or syphilis organisms. From this preliminary screening, Bethune selected some universal donors.

The next day, he drew blood, citrated it, and put it into sterile ampoules. Then, with some needles, rubber tubing, and a helper, he went the short distance to a forward aid station. There he found several soldiers in such desperate condition that the medics were afraid to move them, for fear they would die in transit. With a few ampoules of blood he brought them out of shock and resuscitated them sufficiently so that they could be transported safely to a nearby hospital.

Word of Bethune's life-saving accomplishment passed quickly among the Madrileños. The press and radio trumpeted the event together with an appeal for donors, saying that the laboratory at 36 Principe de Verglara would be open for volunteers in three days. On that third morning, the staff looked out the clinic windows and saw over two thousand people filling the street outside the new lab. And more were arriving all the time. They screened out those younger than eighteen and over fifty. The lab crew took histories, tested for blood type, and drew blood for hours, until all of their containers and refrigerators were full. The donors were given certificates for extra food allotment and, after they rested for ten minutes, a cup of coffee and something to eat. Those not examined wouldn't leave until the lab promised that they would be called upon soon. Those whose blood was taken were told that they could donate not more frequently than once every three weeks.

Thus, with the work of Jorda in Barcelona and the organizing drive of Bethune in Madrid, a modern medical miracle came into being. For the first time it was possible to transfuse wounded soldiers safely near the front; but, as there was no refrigeration at aid stations, blood would not be available there. In our forward hospitals, however, only a kilometer or so back from the front lines, this new miracle worked. This new system, with contributions made by thousands upon thousands of donors, made many surgical procedures feasible and saved countless lives.

In those days, we didn't have the technology to do the complex blood typing and matching that is standard medical practice today. But the simple system of using only those whose blood was in the universal donor category worked extremely well, with relatively few adverse reactions. Apparently, because the blood was from many donors, any elements that might create counterreactions were diluted and thus problems were minimized. I cannot remember ever doing or seeing a direct transfusion (from one person to another) at a forward hospital; even at the base station that method was rarely used. I performed it only a couple of times (during emergencies) at a rear hospital, when the delivery of blood in ampoules had been delayed and when a proper donor (usually someone from a nearby village) was available.

Another major medical development that came from the Republican medical service was the triage system, in which incoming patients were classified according to the seriousness of their injuries. In this approach, the first category were those whose wounds were slight enough that, if necessary, they could wait for treatment. The second group were the seriously wounded, for whom prompt surgical intervention was needed and for whom the prognosis was good. The third and final group were those so seriously wounded that they had little chance for survival no matter what the surgeons might do for them. That group would be the last to be treated.

Triage meant making choices. It may sound like a brutal selection process, abandoning first come–first served, but it did pay off in recovery rates. And this approach is now standard procedure in most armies. It is even used in civilian hospitals treating large numbers of people wounded in natural catastrophes such as earthquakes or hurricanes.

At the beginning of the war, when triage had not yet been established, many men suffering multiple deadly wounds often were taken to the operating table, where the surgical staff spent endless amounts of time, energy, and supplies while the patient slowly died. Meanwhile, other wounded men waiting for treatment got worse, and sometimes died, because they didn't get the prompt surgical intervention that could have saved them. In time of real activity at the front, our medical services were almost always short of supplies and personnel. Even sterile instruments were often in short supply. The limited number of doctors and nurses meant that they often spent such long hours working that their energy sometimes faltered. It made sense to classify the newly arriving cases, even if doing so was heart-rending for both the classifier and the classified.

Very occasionally, I had this triage responsibility, simply because all of the doctors and nurses were in the operating room. To have to look at a patient with chest bandages, for instance, with a depressed blood pressure, seemingly near death, and say that this man should not go ahead of another with a leg wound that could be treated successfully, seemed an impossible task for anyone. It seemed all the more impossible for someone like me, someone without any surgical training. It was like playing God, and I hated it.

Although I kept questioning doctors and nurses about how to make these decisions, I was never comfortable with the judgments I had to make. What was the prognosis for one wound compared with that for another? Was a bullet through the spleen more dangerous than a piece of shrapnel in the liver? Category two? Category three? It was not my problem alone. The doctors and nurses often were uncertain about the decisions they had to make. Fortunately, I did not have to do it very often.

A few years later, when I'd volunteered for service in the U.S. Army during World War II, I had the opportunity, as a medical administrative officer, of lecturing about the Republican wartime medical system to the medical officers at March Field, California. I told them about the triage system, forward placement of hospitals, and the blood transfusion service. The triage system elicited the most questions, with my listeners always wondering how one could make the right decision.

The transfusionist for our Grañen hospital was Dr. Reginald (Reggie) Saxton from England, who was also my superior in the lab. One of the first of the English doctors to arrive, he had first worked on the Aragon front. Slim, tall, blond, and soft-spoken, he taught me much of what I needed to know in the lab and helped in the accumulation of more and better equipment. Later, our little lab was located at the division's base hospital. It had become less primitive over the months and, with his help, I grew in the range of diagnostic tests I could do.

Our lab became increasingly an integral part of our medical service. Soon I was not alone. My first co-worker was an Italian, Ricardo, who came to Spain via the Pasteur Institute in Paris. From under his well-trimmed black beard, which hid his acne-scarred face, he projected a quiet voice and a quick temper. He was a tower of strength, doing both laboratory work and blood transfusions. Ricardo also arranged for the transformation of a large Bedford (British Ford) evacuation ambulance. Its structure had been practically destroyed in a bombing attack, but its engine and chassis were in excellent condition. He oversaw its conversion into a mobile laboratory called an *autochir*. During the first weeks with us, Ricardo spent most of his time at the garage supervising the makeover. When the *autochir* finally arrived, it had a small oven, an autoclave for sterilizing, an incubator for growing cultures, and even more important, a butane-fed refrigerator that allowed us to store blood ampoules. It had enough racks, drawers, and cabinets for the limited extra equipment we had been able to scrounge, plus room for future acquisitions. This new prize meant that we then had to requisition much duplicate equipment, so that when we went up front the base laboratory could remain functioning.

On the dividing wall, just behind the driver's compartment, an upper and lower bunk had been installed for the driver and me to use when we were at a first-line hospital. The height of the compartment was only about five feet, and the width of the bunks was slightly less than twenty inches. A second wall, with a door, separated these bunks from the working part of the *autochir*. This space was so tiny that when we slept there we had to keep the door open or feel suffocated. Nevertheless, it was much better than having to sleep on the ground. Our new mobility allowed us to move up to the front and quickly set up for either lab work or transfusions. The vehicle was soon well enough equipped that I could perform almost all the necessary lab functions. Although there were other *autochirs* in service as mobile operating rooms, and even one as a dental office, ours was the only front-line lab and transfusion service in the army.

With the *autochir* came a driver, Pacho, a former cabby from Valencia. Stocky, powerfully built, with sloping shoulders and a broad, calm face, he was a competent driver, a fair mechanic, and a very helpful addition to the lab service. He knew no English apart from a few curses, so I had to become fluent in Spanish very quickly. Thanks to his help and patience, that went well. But, as he had had only a minimal education, his speech was essentially the language of the streets and often ungrammatical. Consequently, my Spanish suffered the same faults. Upon my return home to UCLA I took a course in Spanish, only to find my grades faltering because of my nearly automatic grammatical mistakes.

Spain was, and is, a land of wine, but we didn't get any very often. Occasionally there was an army issue. On rare occasions it came from the cellar of someone who had crossed over to the Franco side at the outbreak of the war. Since they were "traitors" to the Republic, we didn't have a bad conscience about taking these rarely found caches. Once in a while, one of those liberated bottles was very elegant. More than six decades later, I can still remember with particular relish a thick, sweet, almost syrupy Mólaga, from the mid-nineteenth century, then almost ninety years old.

Almost never were there any white wines. Usually we drank reds from the central seacoast around Valencia or inland from grapes grown on the central plateau east of Madrid. These crudely made young wines, without any bottle age, were harsh with tannins that had not yet softened. But we enjoyed them. Although wine was relatively scarce, we did get some often enough to learn to drink from a *bota,* a leather wine bottle (often made from goat skin, reversed, with the goat hair still inside) or from a *purron,* a glass pitcher with a pouring spout and a hollow handle through which it was filled. The custom with either type of container was that the spout had to be held away from the mouth, never allowed to touch the lips, a sanitary precaution. It became a game when we first started, for often the wine would splash all over our faces. Most of us soon learned how to do it, but sometimes, especially when we had had too much, we missed and had to mop up, to the hilarious ragging of our comrades.

Brandy did a stand-in service for me in place of a dentist. The most primitive of our medical services was dentistry. One American dentist had an *autochir* that was fitted with a treatment chair, foot-pumped drills, and other equipment necessary for taking care of both the preventive and the therapeutic needs of the troops. When the troops were in reserve or the battlefields were quiet, he traveled to the men. But I never saw him. There were probably Spanish dentists, but I don't remember any in our service units, only a couple of dental assistants whose function I never understood.

During the last half of my service, I had a lower molar that had broken off at the gum line and that abscessed every month or so. The dental assistants would take one look at that molar, shake their heads, say that they didn't have the equipment to take care of it, and quickly disappear. So at the first notice of recurrence, the beginning of swelling, I would begin to swallow aspirin to contain the pain—far too many for safety, I suppose, but they let me function for the moment. I would then do all the lab work on hand as fast as possible and make sure that the reserve of blood ampoules was adequate. Then I would make arrangements with one of the hospital doctors to cover the transfusion service for me. When all that was arranged, I went to my bunk in the *autochir* and began to drink brandy until I was numb and passed out. Usually, after a day or so, the swelling would begin to subside and I could come back to work. Now I shudder when I think of the danger of combining the two drugs, alcohol and aspirin. But at that time I was more urgently concerned with blocking out the pain, which was unbearable with the use of aspirin alone. Fortunately, my abscess was patriotic and never acted up when I was at one of the front-line hospitals.

During one period, our hospital was in the Aragon. It was a time when government supplies of all kinds, including food, had been severely limited. We could rarely correlate abundance or scarcity with any events we knew of outside our immediate world. Perhaps it was the harvest, a breakdown in distribution, or the amount of gasoline or number of trucks available for transportation. We never knew.

Our main meal at midday had been almost the same for a couple of weeks. The water that the garbanzos had been cooked in was served as soup, then the garbanzos arrived as the main course, with perhaps a few shreds of onion. The best part of the meal was some bread with olive oil and salt, even though the oil was far from refined. Hungry as we were, it was delicious. Then a kitchen orderly walked around the tables, pausing in front of each of us, counting out exactly three almonds in their shells for our dessert.

The cooking was done over an open fire in large pots almost the size of garbage cans. If the cook were lucky, he would have a few onions and perhaps some garlic cloves for this large batch of chickpeas. One fundamental of cooking garbanzos is that there must be a steady flame, because temperature variation toughens them. But since outside wood fires don't give even heat, we never had tender beans. Another mainstay, and equally unattractive as they were cooked, was lentils, which we derisively called "Dr. Negrín's Victory Pills" (after the president of the Republic).

Somewhere in the midst of this period of culinary scarcity and monotony, someone in our unit had gotten hold of an orange, eaten it privately, and thrown the peel onto the ground right by the entrance to our dormitory, just under the downspout. Frequent rain kept the color of the rind bright for a long time. Each time I came in or went out of the building, I would see that orange peel and begin to drool over the idea of a juicy, sweet orange. While cursing the unknown comrade, the lucky one, for torturing us, somehow I could never make myself pick up the peel and throw it away to end this masochistic punishment. It was almost as if the peel symbolized the importance of good food, especially fresh fruit, of what I desired, what I couldn't have.

CHAPTER 9

Teruel to the Ebro River

Becoming a transfusionist was sudden and accidental. I had been doing blood typing and drawing blood samples for laboratory analysis, so I knew how to get the needle into a vein and draw blood. In fact, I was very good at that, with a highly developed and almost intuitive capacity for locating small, hidden, collapsed veins, or those hidden by fat or muscle. One day at the base hospital, an urgent call for a transfusion came to the lab from the surgical ward. Our supply of blood ampoules had been interrupted, so there were none available. One of the hospital orderlies was sent to find a donor and came back with a young woman, one of the villagers who had volunteered earlier. Up on the ward, I drew a sample from the patient, took it back to the lab, and typed it. Fortunately, she was a universal recipient. Then I checked the donor's blood type and found it be compatible, a universal donor.

Reggie was away; Ricardo was at the garage. There were no doctors available, nor any nurses who wanted to try to do a transfusion. Since there was no one else to do the job, I took the volunteer to the ward, had her lie on a cot next to the patient, set up the equipment, and proceeded with the transfusion. It was a relatively simple one. The soldier's veins were not hidden or collapsed. I was familiar with the equipment, having watched Reggie use it and having cleaned and sterilized it countless times.

As I drew the blood from her and transferred it into him, I kept talking to her.

"*Calma, calma* (be calm, be calm)," I kept repeating. But in fact the words were more for me, inasmuch as she lay there perfectly relaxed. Fortunately, the job was done quickly, and my anxiety turned to pride.

When Ricardo returned, I told him what I had accomplished. He was so scared by what I might have done wrong that he had a fit, bawled me out in Italian, Spanish, French, and English. Reggie, when he came back and heard of my exploit, did the same, although with very, very British reserve. Then, probably in the desperate hope that I wouldn't kill someone in the future, they began to train me. I learned quickly and soon was doing all the transfusions wherever I was stationed. I spent the rest of my time in Spain doing both diagnostic laboratory work and blood transfusions, usually close to the front.

After a relatively short tour of duty with us, Ricardo was transferred and returned to a large base hospital, where his advanced skills and knowledge could be put to better use. After he left, Victor, a volunteer from New York who had more clinical lab experience than I, was assigned to the lab. This meant that I could go to forward installations with our *autochir* whenever action at the front indicated need, while Victor took charge of the base lab. Although I welcomed Victor's help, we never developed a warm relationship. There was no overt friction, but no friendship either. Because he had had some clinical lab experience, he felt that he should be in charge of the lab, but because of my seniority I wasn't about to yield my command position. We probably avoided real conflict only because I was at installations on the front most of the time after his arrival.

In December of 1938, the Republican army headquarters received an intelligence report of an impending large-scale enemy attack on the Guadalajara sector that, if successful, would open the way for Franco to realize his prime goal of seizing Madrid. To divert this action, our high command quickly planned an assault of their own far to the north, with the idea of drawing rebel troops and matériel as far away from Madrid as possible. The focus of our attack was to capture Teruel, the capital of the bleak, rocky province of Aragon.

Action started on December 8 with heavy snow falling. Teruel, in a mountainous region at an altitude of over three thousand feet, was reputed to be the coldest city of the country, and that winter didn't jeopardize its reputation. By New Year's day it was minus 18 degrees F. with winds blowing as high as fifty miles per hour, producing the lowest recorded temperatures of the century. The wind swirled the heavy snowfall so ferociously that at times there was near zero visibility.

The success of the Republican forces in the Teruel operation was due to a combination of surprise, excellent planning, superior troop execution, and the fact that the cold and snow prevented the Franco forces from bringing up their reinforcements quickly or allowing their planes to fly. It was a harsh and bloody operation. The frozen ground defied our attempts to dig in and create adequate defensive positions. Both sides sent patrols out at dawn to cut down telephone poles, which became the prime source of firewood. Coffee froze in cups and blankets were often hard as boards. Many died from exposure.

Six hundred of our supply trucks coming from Valencia were stalled outside of Teruel, unable to enter the city because of the cold and snow. Nevertheless, because we were the attackers, most of our initial supplies were in place, and surprise was on our side. So we not only took the city but made major advances as well. But when the weather moderated, the rebels were able to bring in their heavy artillery and reinforcements, and their planes began to fly sorties. All too soon they dominated the sky, and their big guns could fire with impunity.

By the end of this operation, about fifty thousand enemy troops and more than sixty thousand government soldiers had fallen. As Franco's forces established their superiority in matériel and numbers, they mounted successful counterattacks. Gradually, the Republican troops were forced to retreat to avoid encirclement. It wasn't long before the city was lost once again to the fascists. But the action had achieved its goal of saving Madrid—a costly and bitter victory, as the capital was lost forever a year later.

At the beginning of the war, the International Brigades had acted as a shield against the onslaught of the enemy. Teruel had been the first big Republican victory without us, with the Brigades remaining in reserve positions. The action by the Republican army at Teruel, without the Internationals, proved that it had finally grown from unformed, although heroic, militia units into a disciplined and effective force.

The battle at Teruel, hailed as a Republican victory, was considered the military turning point of the war because it used up such a tremendous portion of the government's supplies of war matériel and the nation's food supplies. Since the main agricultural regions of Spain were in rebel territory, access to food, as well as munitions, was a serious problem. The Non-Intervention blockade had been so effective that our side began to starve for munitions and other supplies, while endless matériel kept pouring in to support the enemy. While the capture of Teruel did prevent a big strike against Madrid, the end of the operation set the stage for the next Franco offensive, which would crash through Aragon and Castellon, down to the Mediterranean, to cut Republican Spain in half.

After the recapture of Teruel, the rebel general staff wanted to mount an immediate push while the Republican forces were in disarray. Franco, to the contrary, ordered a very methodical organization of his forces. This took much longer than seemed actually necessary to his commanders, who had correctly assessed the weakness of our forces. At the time, his strategy seemed incomprehensible. But in a speech that Franco made after the end of the war, he is reported to have said that a rapid end to the war would have left half of the country with its political ideals intact. International wars, he said, concluded with the conquest of enemy territory, but in a civil war, military occupation is not enough—people must be conquered as well. In this case, that meant the Spanish people. This was so important to him that, until the time of his death, he governed the country almost as if it had been occupied by a victorious foreign enemy.

For the Teruel offensive, our forward hospital staff and equipment had been moved to an old stone monastery not many kilometers back from the city. With no beds or cots available, we slept on straw mattresses laid out on the granite floors. In an effort to keep warm, I not only used two straw mattresses for insulation against the cold floor but also kept all my clothes on. One night, after lying on my bed for a half-hour or so, shivering and unable to sleep because of the piercing chill, I went down to the basement, where the morgue was located. Guiding myself by the moonlight that came through a couple of small windows, I went to the nearest corpse and grabbed the blanket covering it. Then I got out of there as quickly as I could and went back to my sleeping area. Using the new blanket as an extra layer kept me just barely warm enough to sleep. While in normal times stealing from a dead man seems repugnant, I felt only a mild twinge of guilt. It seemed so reasonable. The cold would harm me more than it would the cadaver lying two floors below. But it did raise troubling questions about evil and immorality of war. Would I rationalize anything, no matter how vile, just to survive or defeat the enemy?

Once, in the middle of that cold winter, one of the doctors got five of us from the hospital near Teruel together to pool our *pesetas* to pay a farmer and his wife in a nearby farm to kill one of their lambs, roast it, and make us a dinner. Late on a sunny afternoon, we strode about a kilometer through the snow to the farmhouse, quietly but happily chatting about our evening ahead. What a feast it turned out to be! The rare leg of lamb, seasoned with garlic and rosemary from their garden, smelled heavenly as it came out of the oven. The potatoes, fried in olive oil, were crisp around the edges but soft and luscious in the middle. For dessert, we had a marvelous butter cake topped with jam.

It was an extraordinary evening. That simple farmhouse, with the branches of dried rosemary hanging from the wall, the braids of garlic next to them giving off their pungent fragrance, the warmth of a roaring fire, the care our hosts lavished on us, was like an oasis of sanity in a world gone mad. We ate slowly and talked about civilian things: dreams of what we might do when we got home; what the practice of medicine would be like; what it would be like to go to the movies in the evening, or to a good restaurant where we could eat whatever we wanted. We dreamed about a world in which we could order supplies and get them—on time. We savored every moment with joy—the food, the companionship, the warmth of the kitchen, the pleasure of not eating "en masse," but just the five of us: two doctors, two nurses, and me. It was a night to remember—a night that helped us through the months ahead as we dealt once again with bad food, stress, endless work, the mangled and sick bodies, and the all too frequent deaths.

After dinner, seeing a few dried ears of corn hanging in a corner, I tried to bring up the subject of popcorn without knowing the Spanish word for it. My dinner companions, some of whom spoke more Spanish than I, tried to help, throwing in Spanish words they knew, but that only added to the confusion. Finally, with drawings and gestures, we transmitted the idea. At last our host smiled and proudly indicated understanding. I salivated at the idea of finishing this glorious evening by eating a bowl or two of popcorn, a favorite food, before the fire. With pride, the farmer took down one of the dried ears, scraped off five kernels of corn, and threw them onto the hot iron of his wood-burning stove. Then, happily, he handed each of us one kernel of popcorn. Notwithstanding this minor disappointment, as we walked back to the hospital in the moonlight, scuffing through the snow, we were almost floating with a sense of well-being.

No dependable channels existed through which we could get lab material. Our requisitions to the quartermaster service were usually not rejected; they just were not answered. Once, when we heard that a supply depot about fifty kilometers away had some things we needed, Pacho and I decided to drive there. But we couldn't start until well after dinner, after darkness had started to fall. We thought that we would get there, sleep in the *autochir*, get our supplies first thing in the morning, and then get back in time for most of a normal workday.

We had driven past that depot some months before, so we thought we knew how to get there. Road signs didn't exist, however, either because they hadn't been erected or because they had been taken down so that the enemy couldn't use them in case of a breakthrough. And, of course, we had no maps. Driving in the dark on an uncharted highway was frightening, for if we took the wrong road we could end up in enemy territory. So we were both quite tense about directions, worrying about getting captured or shot or killed because we had gone the wrong way.

"Hank, we should go straight ahead."

"No, make a left turn."

"But that will take us into enemy lines."

"No! Go left!"

"But . . ."

"No, I give the orders and I say to go left!"

After arriving safely at the depot, I had a tremendous sense of relief and, as well, a strong confidence in my sense of direction. We slept in the *autochir*, scrounged some breakfast in the morning from their kitchen, and got our supplies. Our drive back in daylight was an easy one.

The problem of getting supplies was ongoing; a broken glass tube could mean that we had to discontinue doing sedimentation tests for weeks. Consequently, we quickly seized every opportunity to enrich our supply of lab equipment or reagents. A report came through that there were medical supplies available in a building on the outskirts of Teruel. Getting matériel from medical installations after an advance meant getting to the city before the enemy counterattack, before the shelling and bombing that would destroy the building and everything within it.

Our forces didn't make many advances, so this was a rare opportunity. Therefore, when the word came, Pacho and I immediately prepared to go. In addition to the supplies we might get, it would be an exciting break in our routine. We bundled up in our warmest clothes and drove there in our *autochir*, arriving after dark. We stopped for information at a large building, an insane asylum on the eastern outskirts of the city. Some troops were gathered outside. It turned out that they were the Lincoln Battalion. From one of the sentries, who seemed to be the only ones awake, we got directions.

It was a weird scene. The off-duty Lincolns were huddled around a series of bonfires, wrapped in blankets, trying to keep from freezing. This was the time before radar, and so planes rarely flew at night, although occasional night bombings were made on the largest cities, such as Madrid, Valencia, or Barcelona. But even those were done mainly when the moon was out, so that the bombardiers could locate their targets. This meant that the light of the bonfires gave away nothing to enemy planes, and the building itself blocked the light to enemy gunners to the west.

Thick snow covered the ground. The huge brick building partially shielded the Lincolns from the direct force of the wind, but the flames of the fires jumped about, sending massive moving shadows of men and tree branches onto the walls. The colors of this bivouac area were stark black and white, punctuated only by the flickering orange of the fires. The only sound was that of the firewood snapping.

The mother superior with her six nuns, many acolytes, and patients were holed up inside the asylum, terrified that the "Bolsheviks" outside were about to break in to rape and kill them. Spanish-speaking Commissar Keller of the Lincolns, a non-communist and a practicing Catholic, was inside, trying to get the mother superior to evacuate to a safe place. He was trying to convince her that she and her charges would be well taken care of if she allowed us to take them out of danger. The real danger, he told her, would come from shelling from the expected Franco counter-offensive, which would surely destroy the building. Although the Dominicans were frightened and wary of the Lincolns, they allowed themselves to be transported to a building far to the east, down on the coast below Valencia. Shortly thereafter, the building in Teruel was heavily bombed and shelled by the Franco forces.

From time to time, one of the inmates would appear in a window, grimacing and gesticulating wildly. Occasionally one would dart outside, only to be pulled back quickly by one of the attendants. It was almost like a stage setting from an operatic tragedy. The scene utterly transfixed me and, oblivious of the cold, I stood staring for a long while until Pacho pulled me away.

Pacho drove our *autochir* a few hundred feet south, to the building we had been looking for. There, he forced open the door on the street side of the building with a tire iron. There wasn't much for us on the ground floor, which was mainly a reception desk and some offices, but upstairs was a treasure vault. The windows on the west, away from the street, faced the enemy, so we felt literally under the gun, sensing that bullets might come crashing through the windows at any time. Using only two small lanterns and working carefully behind the walls, we hoped that we would be shielded from enemy view. When we had to pass those western windows, we crawled under them, pushing our lanterns along the floor. Somehow, the possibility of danger and the quiet affected both of us so that we whispered to each other, even though there was no need for silence.

"Take this?" Pacho would ask.

"Don't need," would be my terse whisper, or a simple "Yes."

We found all sorts of equipment: microscopes, incubators, test tubes, petri dishes and other laboratory glassware, a microtome, chemicals, reagents, stains. There were many items that I didn't recognize, but if they would fit into the *autochir* I took them anyway, figuring that someone would know what they were and how to use them. Several hours later, we had loaded all that we could pack into the back of our *autochir,* even jamming the sleeping compartment and bunks full. The laboratories in the building were pretty well emptied. Then we drove back through the night to our base, arriving early in the morning, exhausted but exhilarated.

As we excitedly unloaded and sorted through our haul later that day, it became clear that much of what we had found was more advanced or complicated than our own simple lab could use. Some duplicated what we already had. Whenever an ambulance was going that way and had some space, we shipped the excess equipment to Ricardo for his base hospital lab. As for us, we now had all the equipment we needed to do almost anything the medical staff asked of us.

About six months after Teruel, word came again to our general staff of another planned enemy advance. In an attempt to forestall it, once again our side made a preemptive move. At one in the morning of the July 25, 1938, the Republican forces, under the command of General Vicente Rojo, one of the few high-ranking army officers loyal to the Republic, crossed the Ebro River along a front twenty-five miles long. It was the last of the offensive actions in which the International Brigades were involved and, indeed, was the last major offensive by the Republican army. Within three days our troops had penetrated about fifteen miles into enemy territory, seizing five hundred square miles and capturing four thousand prisoners. It was an action that tied up the insurgent army for about four months and diverted a rebel attack on Valencia, only ninety miles away.

To start the offensive, small boats had been secretly carried at night on trolleys over very rough terrain to the banks of the Ebro River. Eighty thousand men had been transferred to the area. Because the permanent bridges over the river had been bombed, small pontoon bridges were hidden near the eastern bank of the river for the initial push. These were lightweight, capable of carrying only men, not trucks or ambulances. Stronger structures came a few days later.

As the days of the offensive passed and our troops moved forward, a few trucks were ferried over, which were immediately put to double duty. After delivering their supplies to the front, they collected the wounded and brought them back to the river. After a ride in these jolting trucks, the *heridos* (wounded) had to be carried by bearers on foot over the pontoon bridges to ambulances waiting on the eastern bank that could then take them to the forward hospitals. Often the wounded had to lie on their litters or on the ground for hours, shaken by bombings, choking on dust, waiting to be taken across the river. Yet nothing could be done for them until the action quieted for a moment or until destroyed pontoons could be replaced. By the time they reached us, they were most often in some extra degree of shock.

The terrain of the Sierra Pandols over which the troops were fighting was so steep and treacherous that often the wounded were brought down to aid stations by bearers on *artolas* (litters designed to be carried on mules). And sometimes the ground was so difficult to traverse or so open to enemy fire that the only way to bring out a wounded man was piggyback on a bearer. One of the first jobs of the battalion and station medics was to scour the captured territory for any stray mules, mule carts, or *artolas*. At one point, the advanced medical transportation for the Lincolns consisted of four mules, two carts, and three *artolas*.

It wasn't until days later that bridges (actually large-scale pontoons) were erected so that ambulances could go all the way to and from the front. Dr. Pike had to bully the engineers to fashion a road closer to where the Lincolns were fighting, so that ambulances could come close and lessen the trek required of the bearers.

After our initial advance, the enemy mobilized a force of 300,000 for the counterattack. In addition to far outnumbering us, they also had overwhelming superiority of arms and an almost absolute control of the air. After the successful surprise and our first quick penetration, the calls on the battlefield of *"Ayuda!"* or *"Socorro"* (help) or *"Practicante!"* (aid man!) never seemed to stop. Casualties began streaming back to our hospitals in a flood.

Our first forward hospital of the offensive was located in a large but relatively shallow cave about a kilometer or so back from the Ebro River. Its stone floor was partitioned into various rooms by curtains strung on wires: a surgical ward, recovery room, patients' area, and even sleeping quarters, although few of us had much time for sleep. As the battle progressed, the ambulances arrived at the cave in a steady stream from river's edge. Later they began coming directly from aid stations located inside the zone of the advance. Day and night they poured in; the field of stretchers seemed to expand every hour. The wounded on their stretchers were placed at the forward, open face of the cave, and at times this collection of wounded extended beyond the sheltering overhang. Fortunately, it didn't rain, nor were we attacked by enemy aircraft.

Halfway through the first really busy day, I both had to give transfusions and perform triage. I began to sort out and classify the men, giving transfusions to those who needed it most. When the operating room finished with a case, two orderlies would carry the patient on a stretcher to a bed, where the ward nurses took over. Then the next wounded man was taken into surgery in the order I had established.

On one stretcher I came across Paine, one of my comrades from the Mackenzie-Papineau Battalion who, back home in Everett, Washington, had been an aviator. We had not had a particularly intimate relationship, but as he was from the West Coast and from my former battalion, I felt close to him and distressed by his condition. Seeing him stirred the guilt I felt of not being on the firing line. I still have a snapshot of Paine sent to me by his sister after I came home. It shows him standing in the snow in front of his home, dressed in a fur-lined flier's outfit, tall and slim, handsome, with blond hair and somewhat craggy features. He had come to Spain to fly, but we had so few planes that he had ended up fighting in the infantry.

When I first noticed him, he was so seriously hurt, with two bullet wounds in his chest and one in his head, that I automatically had to classify him in group three. Blood had seeped through the chest bandages and was still flowing, red and fresh. There was a smell emanating from him that said "death." Contrary to established triage procedure, and to what my head told me as well, I transfused him. Then a short time later I gave him another ampoule. Twice more I tried to rally him sufficiently so that I could legitimately ask surgery to try to save him. It was a waste of precious blood, because his wounds were so wide open that the blood leaked out almost as fast as I could put it in. He was beyond help, and after an hour or so I had to pull the blanket over his head and the bearers took him outside for burial.

A couple of days later, when the immediate push was over and work slackened, I gave myself permission to experience my feelings. I wrote a long poem about his life and death. It was my lament for the dying. It was the last poem I ever wrote. Now I have only the first part of it:

From far away
From Everett on the Puget Sound
With the peace of its water
The serenity of its green hills
You came from so far
To a dusty plain, to mountains without peace.

You expected to fly
To strike the enemy boldly from the sky
Guns roaring
Your strong hands guiding your plane,
Triggering your guns.

Instead you had to fight on foot.
Did you ever expect to die?
To have a bullet in your head?
To suffer your guts torn apart?

And was it worth it?
Was the pain too much?
Was there even pain for you?
Was the cost of death too high?

Some days later, another wounded soldier came to the cave. He too was classified as group three. He was unconscious, barely showing any vital signs, and had no identification on him. Because the army issued no dog tags, we never knew who he was. But he was not an International, for the few barely coherent words he whispered seemed to be in Catalan. There had been a lull in admissions when he arrived, and the operating room was free, so he was taken almost immediately into surgery. The doctors repaired his torn body as best they could, but that meant only that they tied blood vessels, sewed up wounds, and patched a bit. It was like putting band-aids on a serious heart injury.

Nobody in the medical staff doubted that he would die in a few days, or a week at the very most. Meanwhile, he lay in constant, agonizing pain, as we did not have enough morphine to keep him fully sedated. All of us, nurses, doctors, and orderlies, tried to make his last hours easier for him. We would mop his brow, try to move his one remaining leg to a more comfortable position, change the placement of his wounded arms, sometimes sneaking him a shot of morphine. Nothing we could do helped very much. His constant cries and moans were traumatizing to other patients who were trying to contain their own pain. His condition, too critical to permit evacuation back to a base installation, was deteriorating rapidly. His outcries became louder, more frequent, and more plaintive.

Our helplessness made us all feel guilty. His moans and screams cut into me so that even when I left the cave for a break, I could hear his cries no matter how far away I walked. After a couple of days, his blood pressure dropped dangerously low, his general condition deteriorated, and his pain seemed to worsen. The surgeons said that he would die in two days at the outside; there was nothing they could do. But I felt a need to do something, anything. I debated with myself, arguing back and forth. After much agonizing, and without consulting anyone, I went to his bed when no one else was on the ward. I sterilized his skin on the inside of his elbow—an absurd ritual, as I was about to kill him—then I injected enough air into his vein to end his life immediately. In that moment, I was so connected with him that we seemed to be taking the same labored breaths, breathing as one. He stopped breathing; I held my breath for what seemed long minutes. He breathed again, a couple of swift inhalations, then stopped for good. Only then could I breathe once again.

I had killed him! It was painless and merciful. So I told myself. But I was soon having second thoughts about playing God. I knew I had done the humane thing, but the questions remained, still remain. Did I have the right? Because I had made the decision alone, I felt I couldn't share my doubts and angst with anyone. To this day, whenever I think about it my stomach tightens and does nip-ups, but I am convinced not only that I would do this act of mercy again, but that I would want someone to perform the same service for me.

While getting a needle into a vein for a transfusion is relatively easy under normal circumstances, our situation was anything but normal. The wounded were usually in some degree of shock, so that their blood vessels were frequently semicollapsed, which made finding entry into the vein very difficult. Very often I had to do it prior to surgery as part of a pre-op workup in the hope of increasing the patient's chances for survival. But it was not usually done at bedside or in the operating room. Rather, most of the time I knelt on the ground next to the stretcher, working in poor light.

The problem was compounded by the fact that the only needles we had available had a relatively large bore, making them extremely difficult to get into the vein. And since they were a precious commodity, I had to use and reuse them, meaning that I had to sharpen them on a whetstone. They were never as good as the occasional new ones we got, no matter how skilled I became at sharpening. A couple of times the shock to the person's system was so profound that his veins were completely collapsed. Then I would have to cut with a scalpel and dissect the wounded soldier's arm before I could expose the vein to get the needle in and start the transfusion.

Maintaining a sterile atmosphere in such a situation was almost impossible. I would wash my hands as thoroughly as possible, but sometimes there wasn't much water. A quick alcohol hand rinse followed. Then I would come back with my sterile scalpel and tincture of iodine to sterilize the patient's skin. To do the job I had to kneel in the dirt, with no assistant to hand me the scalpel or needle. If the patient moved or twitched, the gear, often of necessity balanced on his chest, could slide to one side or onto the ground, and that would be the end of sterility.

Our work in the hospital reflected the battlefront. When casualties were heavy our work never stopped, day or night. At one point in the Ebro offensive the entire staff of the hospital worked for three days and three nights straight before the influx of wounded slackened. At times like that, we did our job on automatic pilot, working on nerve alone.

After that extended episode, when the stream of arriving wounded had slowed, I went to my bunk in the *autochir* and lay down without undressing. Asleep in moments, I was soon dreaming that I was doing transfusions. In my dream, however, my left hand was holding an ampoule of blood high over my head and the blood from that ampoule went into my hand. I held another ampoule in my right hand, straight out in front of me, and blood went from me into that ampoule and then poured out in a huge stream onto the floor. The imagery was so strong that I woke in a sweat, feeling that all the transfusions I had done were worthless, that I was just pouring life onto the floor. I couldn't calm down enough to sleep again, so I got up and went outside, standing bleary-eyed in the sunlight. Elizabeth, a British surgical nurse, came by, also wound up tight and unable to sleep. The two of us walked into an adjoining field and sat under an olive tree. Her feet were so swollen from the hours of standing in the operating room that I gently rubbed them to ease her pain. We sat for an hour or so, sometimes talking, more often silent, before we could unwind enough to sleep.

Being a medical technician, working in this pressured hospital setting, made my fantasy of being a novelist fade into the background. Writing was something I did only in letters home, not as a vision of my future. I began leaning more and more toward finishing my premedical studies and becoming a doctor. But the idea of going back to school for five or more years for medical training was in competition with my intensifying antifascist feelings. And the idea of becoming politically active, perhaps doing political work full-time, was growing within me.

One day, Ted, the doctor who was the head of our hospital, took me out for a walk. Putting his arm over my shoulders, he said, "Hank, you and your unit have done such a good job for us, and you've built such a good organization, that I have just put the papers through to commission you a *teniente* (lieutenant) and to promote Pacho to *cabo* (corporal). I've checked, and it looks as if there will be no obstacles to having it approved. It was a real pleasure to do this. Congratulations."

Wearing a wide grin, I walked back to the hospital with him, where a group of the staff, who had been told of my promotion, greeted me with applause, shouting "*Viva el teniente!*" This recognition helped to dispel my lurking feeling of guilt that I was not at the front, a feeling that until then had never completely left me. Although I was thereafter treated as an officer and thought of myself as one, the formal papers commissioning me did not get back to our division before we were repatriated a few months later. So, officially, I was listed and paid as a *soldado* to the end. Some sixty years later, when the records of the International Brigade came back from the former Soviet Union, where they had been taken for safekeeping and then buried, I learned that my commission had been approved.

To keep our service as close to the action as possible and to minimize the time between injury and treatment, we moved forward, across the Ebro and upstream to just below the pueblo of Flix. This pueblo did not have any buildings large enough to accommodate us, but just downstream was a large hill that extended all the way to the river's edge. It had been tunneled with a bore large enough for the railroad's double tracks. As no trains were running at that time, we could set up our hospital inside. The mass of the hill was great enough so that not too much dirt drifted down, even from occasional direct bomb hits.

On the village side, a small area had been leveled off in front of the entrance to the tunnel so that an ambulance could come and discharge or pick up patients. They were not allowed to remain any longer than necessary, for that would have been an advertisement to enemy planes to come and attack. Pacho drove our *autochir* some distance away into a tree-covered area and left it there. During that period my work was almost entirely as a transfusionist, there being little demand for me to do any clinical tests. I had a cot in the tunnel.

At the entrance to the tunnel, a high, triple row of sandbags had been erected in the form of a large S to serve as a protective shield against shrapnel from bomb bursts. The barrier was constructed with its walls wide enough apart so that the stretcher bearers could easily turn when carrying the wounded. At the other end of the tunnel, a similar set of sandbags had been set in place. Just inside the tunnel was the receiving room; past that, hanging curtains formed a cramped surgery, which had been leveled off with planking. The next area held the patients' cots. We placed the beds at right angles to the rails, leveling them with railroad ties. The cots for the personnel were at the other end, screened off from the patients, with a separate section for nurses.

We at the hospitals ate better than they did in the infantry, if for no other reason than that our supplies could be delivered more easily and our cooks didn't have to transport the cooked food forward, as they did for the front lines. Nevertheless, the food was never very good, and occasionally it was very bad.

Cooking for the hospital was done just outside the back entrance to the tunnel. The cook had metal stands that held his pots and frying pans over the wood fires. There I was introduced to paella. Our new cook was a Valenciano who knew how to cook his regional rice dish very well. He had somehow gotten some meat, even a small amount of ham, the first I had tasted since coming to Spain. There were some onions, and, of course, rice and some saffron to give the dish its distinctive flavor and aroma. He even had the traditional large, thin, shallow iron paella pan, which he must have carried with him wherever he was stationed.

Word had spread that our new cook's first lunch was to be some special treat, so everyone who could get away from his immediate duties was standing near the kitchen a little before noon. We eagerly sniffed the aromas of meat, onions, and saffron, and salivated in anticipation. Unfortunately, lunch that day happened to coincide with one of the frequent midday bombings. With the first explosions, everyone, the cook staff included, quickly retreated into the tunnel behind the sandbag walls. Everyone, that is, except me. I crouched down, piling a plate high with the rice and meat dish. I then lay flat, on the side of the railbed near the paella pan, and stuffed myself with this marvelous creation. The kernels of rice were whole and firm but just tender enough, richly yellow from the saffron and suffused with the flavor of the herb.

Occasionally, in the short pauses between flights of bombers, I would lift myself up to the large, blackened paella pan, sniff it once again to savor the spiciness, and refill my plate, thinking it would be bad enough to die, but to die on an empty stomach and miss food this good would be a major catastrophe.

CHAPTER 10

Benicasim back to UCLA

Not long after our foray into Teruel for equipment, I was transferred to a hospital on the Mediterranean coast about twenty miles north of Barcelona. After a week or so of doing nothing there, I was bored to death and protested to the hospital administration that this was a wasted assignment. They agreed, and a short time later I was reassigned to the laboratory at the International Brigade base hospital in Benicasim on the Mediterranean coast just north of Valencia. The hospital, located on a calm and beautiful beach, had been an elegant resort hotel before the war. In this setting, the war seemed far away. But we were always jostled back to the realization of war's grisly detritus as the soldiers with their horrible wounds descended upon us in a never-ending stream.

The medical personnel of this hospital were, for the most part, not members of the armed forces. Rather, they were a unit of the International Sanitary Service (ISS). The ISS staffed some twenty-five hospitals in Spain, fielding volunteers that included 220 doctors, 550 nurses, and 600 ambulance drivers, stretcher bearers, and first-aid personnel. They were responsible for a total of five thousand beds and fourteen surgical groups. While they served all the sick and wounded of the army, they were the main source of treatment for the International Brigades. As the war progressed, the Brigades were increasingly composed of Spanish soldiers. Casualties among the Brigaders, combined with a diminishing influx of Internationals, made this changing composition almost inevitable. By the time I was assigned there, but not to the ISS, almost 80 percent of its beds were filled by wounded Spaniards.

This international organization raised funds around the world, sent out volunteers, and governed their comings and goings. One hundred and fifty ambulances either came to Spain with accompanying medical staff or were bought with money donated abroad. Although the French government interdicted other matériel, it did allow medical supplies and personnel to pass the border. Medical personnel had volunteered from twenty-two nations. The American Hospital Group, developed under the direction of Dr. Edward Barsky, had three units: the one in Benicasim and two others, one in the Madrid sector and the other in the south of Spain.

The work at the Benicasim laboratory kept me quite busy but was never overwhelming. There were few emergencies that required long hours or night assignments, and I had no transfusion duties, for the hospital had its own staff for that service. Our food was noticeably better than in the forward positions, and I put back a few more of my lost pounds. I regularly spent a portion of my pay on the easily available and delicious blood oranges that were local to the area. There was always a bag of them in the lab, and I dipped into it so often that I had frequent diarrhea again. After months of being deprived of fresh fruit, I couldn't make myself stop eating them.

Two bright spots highlighted that relatively short Mediterranean assignment: music and sex. And to this day I don't know which was more important.

Music came first, when I fell in love with the sound of the cello.

One Sunday afternoon, the world-renowned Catalan cellist Pablo Casals gave a concert for the hospital staff and a few ambulatory patients. This was, I believe, his last trip to his homeland for several decades. During the war, he spent most of his time and energy raising money and gathering support for Spain in lands around the world. After Franco won, he publicly announced that he would not return to the rule of the dictator. In protest, he made a new home in Puerto Rico, teaching cello and occasionally giving a concert.

The deep, complex notes from his cello began my love affair with the instrument that is with me still. I had known cello music but had never really seriously attended to it before, at least not with the joy I experienced that day. The low tones seemed to pulse inside me. When played alone, the violin creates beautiful music, but I appreciate it in a more intellectual way. The viola is more sensuous than the violin, and the string bass seems just a bit too low, except when played with other instruments. Only the cello fully resonates to my personal vibrations.

Classical music had always moved me, so this concert wasn't a new experience. I had even heard the pieces that Casals played that day, some of them many times. While on the UCLA campus, I had spent countless lunch hours listening to the noon organ concerts in Royce Hall. The weekly broadcasts of the New York Philharmonic were my favorite radio programs. My parents knew that if they wanted to reward or bribe me, the best gift they could give was a ticket to a concert at the Hollywood Bowl. It isn't the intricacy or brilliant complexity of a composition that catches me, but the flow of the sound, the movement, the feelings they generate inside, As a student, I had written many poems trying to capture what a particular performance meant to me. Chamber music was my special favorite. Complex but not overwhelming in structure, it reached deep inside me.

Before that Casals concert, for months the only sounds I had heard had been the grinding, exploding uproar of war—trucks discordantly shifting their gears, the clanking of tanks, the moans and cries of the wounded, the crash of falling buildings, exploding bombs, artillery and antiaircraft guns firing, planes droning overhead or whining as they dove down on us. To find myself one day in that large, windowed, porchlike room with sunshine streaming in, the green limbs of trees swaying outside, and the music filling all the spaces inside was wondrous indeed.

The great virtuosity and intensity that imbued Casals's music sent a personal message to me that lasts to this day. The instrument seemed almost as big as that small man. He held it tenderly but firmly, almost as if it were his lover. The melodies of that afternoon sang a romantic refrain for me.

Jack, an ISS ambulance driver in his middle thirties, sat next to me during the concert. Before volunteering he had been second violinist with the Rochester, New York Symphony Orchestra. He sat entranced, almost rigid, his face crinkled and tears streaming down his cheeks. Only his fingers resting on his lap were moving, as they played the notes along with Casals.

I sat, virtually immobilized, yet I felt as if I were dancing inside. Even now, whenever I hear the Brahms Double Concerto, which Casals played that wonderful, Sunday afternoon, my eyes tear and my throat constricts. Playing without the accompanying instruments the music calls for, he made the composition sound whole. As great a musician as Casals was, I have no doubt that my own need for beauty, for some sanity, made me receptive to the music in ways that I'd never experienced before. After the concert, I wandered alone up and down the beach for about an hour, listening to the soft sounds of the surf, savoring the moment, feeling quietly at peace and far away from strife.

Sensory deprivation, particularly in the realm of food and drink, was very real. But all through this year and a half of bombing and guns, I was even more worried about dying a virgin than about dying. And I was a virgin until late in the war. It may be incomprehensible today for a healthy, virile young man to be a virgin at the age of twenty-two, when neither religion nor other moral scruples stood in the way. But in those long-ago days before the pill and the sexual revolution, virginity in either sex was not that rare. Can you imagine an urban, eighteen-year-old college student today worrying that she might become pregnant because she had sat on the lap of her boyfriend while they were kissing and fondling one another, both fully clothed the entire time? That happened to me with my friend Ruth. And we were not alone in our ignorance and innocence.

The few young Spanish women I met had a practical philosophy that was quite startling to me. It was summed up as *Habla, pero no me toca*, Speak but don't touch me. One could speak in the most suggestive manner without serious offense, but the slightest touch was forbidden. Other comrades, truthfully or not, told of more successful encounters with women who were not prostitutes. Perhaps because of my innocence—or maybe just my ineptitude—I got *Habla, pero no me toca*.

Actually, the sex drive of the men in our unit during my training period was rather ephemeral. A combination of a low-protein diet, high heat, frequent diarrhea and dysentery, and lots of grueling exercise zapped our libidos. We dreamed and talked more about food than about sex. We would discuss our favorite dishes, how to cook them, which were the best ingredients, the finest restaurants. These were constantly and interminably the subjects of our conversation—a not uncommon phenomenon in wartime. When I was in basic training with the machine gun company, an erection upon awakening was such an infrequent event that the man who had one would cover his genital area with his helmet and yell "Tent! Tent!" and everyone would stand at attention and offer a mock salute. Later on, when out of basic training, our urges were not so remote.

The only alternatives to abstinence were masturbation or a visit to a prostitute. Such a visit was contrary to my political and moral beliefs, as it was for most of my comrades. If there were camp followers, I didn't see them where we were stationed. Of course there were women working the trade, but they were mainly in the urban areas, and leaves to the cities were very rare. Later in the war, the Republican Army institutionalized the practice of granting formal leaves of thirteen days, but only after six months at the front.

My single experience with a prostitute was in Barcelona, where I had gone a second time to get some supplies and equipment, this time with our *autochir*. Pacho had a local girlfriend (he seemed to have them everywhere), so he was away for the night. Determined to end my virginity that evening, I wandered up and down the Ramblas de Las Flores, the prostitutes' working street, trying to screw up my courage. I watched as the women made contact, disappeared with their tricks into dingy hotels on the side streets, and reappeared not very long afterward. It took more than an hour before I could make myself approach one of the women and communicate my desire. She was a young, attractive woman with her clothes cut to show off her slim figure and prominent breasts. Her stance and walk matter-of-factly advertised her profession.

I took her to the *autochir*, which was parked a short block away, so we would not have to sneak into a dirty hotel room. When she took off her dress, I saw black, cotton underwear. While black, lacy lingerie back home had always been very attractive and erotically stimulating to me, black cotton had become just the opposite for me since coming to Spain. The common uniform for farming and factory women was a somewhat formless black dress that never seemed to be quite clean and was certainly not attractive. The combination of her black cotton underwear, her casual, business-as-usual approach, and my ignorance and fear of disease left me embarrassingly impotent. Even when her hands guided mine over her breasts and thighs, the excitement of feeling her lovely body didn't arouse me sufficiently.

She tried her best and got me half started, but it just didn't work. Finally, in agony, I paid her the agreed amount plus a generous tip and apologized for not being able to perform. I still believe that the shame of paying for something that should result only from shared desire was a central factor in my impotence. The idea of buying what should be given in affection was just as repugnant to me as would have been taking it by force.

My fear of venereal disease was even a stronger deterrent. Venereal diseases were not just frightening ailments I had heard described in a lecture or had read about in texts. During our hike across the Pyranees, I had seen the agony Ed suffered with his gonorrheal arthritis. Moreover, while I was working as a research assistant for Dr. Bailey in the Bacteriology Department at Los Angeles City College, my professor was doing experimental work on staining the spirochete that caused syphilis. One of my assignments was to go downtown to the Los Angeles City Venereal Disease Clinic to make slides for his experiments. That meant that, with a piece of gauze, I had to take an infected penis in my hand, hold it so that the chancres were exposed, and then, with a cotton swab, take some fluid to smear on glass slides. It was frightening, even wearing rubber gloves, and a vivid reminder of the cost of sexual carelessness.

When my "rented woman" had left, I got into my bunk and breathed a sigh of relief. Then I cried with a mixture of shame and pain and sadness and desire. I was still a virgin.

But my posting to Benicasim would soon take care of that. Throughout my time there, I had enjoyed the companionship of Anna, a Canadian nurse. I had first noticed her sitting on the opposite side of the room at the Casals concert, attractive, graceful, with a lovely smile when she turned to the person next to her. We met one afternoon when she was the assisting nurse at a minor operation a doctor performed on one of my fingers, which had become infected. Our relationship started one evening in the staff lounge. I was reading, and she and two others were looking for a fourth for bridge. No one else was around, so I became their candidate. I pleaded ignorance, never having played the game before. But they insisted that they could teach me quickly. In a few minutes they had instructed me in the rules and procedures of the game, how to count tricks and how to bid. We started playing. In the first hand I bid one no trump and then she rebid it up to a grand slam in no trump. Because together we had such good cards, we made it. I thought we should stop playing after that, as we had reached the top, and I didn't expect a repeat performance. But they prevailed and the game continued for several hours more.

Several nights later Anna came down to the lab to see me as I was finishing an urgent blood analysis. We chatted for about an hour while I finished the test, wrote up the results, and cleaned the equipment. When everything was put away, our talk became more personal. Suddenly she reached over and gently caressed my cheek with one finger, then cupped my chin in her hand and held it there for a moment. With her eyes and her hand she told me that she wanted me. Her hand also told me that I should not charge ahead, but let her set the pace.

It was a quiet moment as she held me. Because she was at least ten years older than I and experienced, I was glad to let her guide me. Although wild with desire, I worried that I might have misread her invitation, confused simple friendliness for a sexual invitation. I needed her help to slow myself down. I was so unsure, so frightened, so needy. She handled my awkwardness easily, until finally I could relax into the unfolding mystery of exploring her body and the delight of my own responses.

While Anna was able to give me tenderness and love, she also made clear that she neither offered nor expected any deep, long-term, emotional commitment. At first I couldn't understand. If this was so wonderful, why couldn't we be partners, planning a future together? It took a while for me to accept that we could share physical pleasure and caring and loving tenderness without thinking about a future. As a result, when it came time for me to leave for the front once again, it was not the heart-rendering anguish of one-sided love, just sadness that something so lovely was ending. She gave me so much more than the release of tension and liberation from the fear of dying a virgin. I learned from her how to give and to take in a mutually loving exchange. Not long ago, when reading of her death in her native Canada, I offered a deep, silent thanks to her once again for a most gracious and generous friendship.

Although I was able to do lab work and contribute to the functioning of the hospital, there wasn't any urgent need here for my services. I had been sent away from our unit during a lull in the fighting, in a period of organizational reshuffling of the medical services. When the reorganization that had sent me from the 35th Division Medical Services was completed a couple of months later, I went back to the 35th Division main hospital. Again, in the way of all armies, it was without any consultation with me, just the anonymous orders that are the essence of army procedure. Leaving Benicasim was difficult because of Anna. Nor was the softness of living with a real bed (actually a cot in a room of my own) and good food that easy to give up. But being where my services would be better utilized compensated me, at least in part, for those losses. I wanted and needed to be back where I was more useful.

By this time, I had been in Spain a little more than a year, and my language facility was pretty good. I was fluent, if not always grammatically correct. During a lull in operations, several of the hospital orderlies and drivers had asked me to teach them to speak English. Eight of us formed a class that I taught for the next several weeks.

Prior to the Republic, almost half the Spanish population was illiterate, so education had become a matter of pressing civic urgency. One of the first governmental actions had been the establishment of schools throughout the country, from the tiniest, poorest villages to the front lines. The lack of appropriate textbooks was a crucial problem for the new government. Most of those that had been used previously were unacceptable because they had been written by the church and were, essentially, composed of the catechism. But schools and classes were quickly set up, and elementary texts were printed to start a major attack on illiteracy.

The members of our group were literate, but we did not have any books on how to teach or speak English as a second language. And I had no idea of how to teach a language class. We started in a cooperative way. They helped me to teach them. Most of them were quite facile and caught on very quickly, more quickly, in fact, than I had learned Spanish. But we encountered a major problem with the pronunciation of certain words, because of what they had learned over the months in contact with various Brigaders.

"YEW RUN A LA *BOR* A TOREE," said Juan, accenting the fifth syllable.

"NO! NO!" corrected Gallego, *"LAB* OR A TOREE," putting the accent on the first syllable before I could say anything.

Both were absolutely certain they were right, because they had good ears and were excellent mimics. One had learned the word from an English ambulance driver with an Oxford accent, the other from an English doctor from Cambridge whose pronunciation of the word was different. Teaching English was complicated by the fact that Miguel, one of the members of the class, had been working with a mechanic from London who in typical cockney fashion dropped the beginning *H,* saying "arry" for "Harry." But when he came to Spain and learned some Spanish, which often drops the beginning *H,* he would pronounce it. For example, he would pronounce the word *habla,* "to speak," sounding the beginning *H.* In Spanish it is dropped. The students fought among themselves about the correct way to speak, but their squabbling only seemed to make the class more interesting. I tried to explain the differences in English pronunciation to them by comparing these variances to the wide range of pronunciations and dialects in Spain, such as the lisp that is natural in many parts of the country but not others. Still, they were not quite satisfied with my explanation; they fervently wanted to speak only the "correct" English.

The class ended when a new round of activity at the battlefront meant that I had to go to a forward hospital, but I heard later that several of the students met together for quite a while afterward, teaching themselves. In the process of teaching English, my Spanish became better. When I returned to Los Angeles, I was actually able to make short speeches in Spanish about the war.

It was not just my facility with the language that was growing. I had also learned about the country with which I had allied myself. Shut off from Western Europe by the Pyrenees, Spain was distinct in more than just geography. In 1931, at the inception of the Republic, industrial capitalism was still in its infancy, with considerable remnants of feudalism still prominent. Spain was then predominantly an agrarian country with a very diverse agriculture. The controlling economic and political forces were the *latifundists* (the large landowners), the clergy, the monarchy, and the army. They might disagree among themselves, mount coups against each other to take power, even murder one another, but they would quickly unite in opposition to any threats from below.

We Americans are imbued with the concept that while we might have deep conflicts on political and social issues, these struggles will be peacefully expressed and resolved. But this war in Spain was the country's fourth bloody military conflict since the early nineteenth century, a period of little more than a hundred years. In fact, the history of Spain has been described as a thousand years of civil wars. Attempts at fundamental reform had always been met by violent reactionary repression. Elections were controlled or rigged. Challenges to the system that did arise in local areas were routinely and brutally suppressed.

It was hard for me to grasp the degree of control the government had had over this country before the Republic. The rulers' disregard of the needs and wishes of those who were below them, and their commitment to destroy any movement that threatened their domination, were almost impossible for me as an American to comprehend or accept. "Free speech" was not an acceptable phrase in the ruling vocabulary. It was no surprise that the great changes wrought by the Republic would be resisted so ferociously.

The unfortunate reality was that after the capture and loss of Teruel and the crossing of the Ebro, the war was drawing to a close, with the Franco forces winning. Dr. Juan Negrin, the prime minister of Spain, went to Geneva to the League of Nations. On September 21, 1938, twenty-six months after the start of the revolt, he announced that in the interest of lessening the strife between nations and preventing war in Europe, his government was suggesting that both sides withdraw all of the Internationals in their service. His government, he said, would do so unilaterally. When he asked that an international commission be sent from the League to supervise this withdrawal, he was greeted with great applause. The other side, of course, did not agree to withdraw their "volunteers."

Indeed, the fascist representatives had made proposals for mutual withdrawal almost from the beginning of the war. In discussions at the League and in the Non-Intervention Commission, Italy and Germany had also spoken in this vein. At first, when they expected a quick victory, they suggested withdrawals after three months. This quickly changed to six months. Finally, their agreement was conditioned on the border being hermetically sealed and the government—which for them, of course, meant the Burgos government of Franco—being in control. Each time the Italian or German representatives at the League or in the Non-Intervention Commission raised the withdrawal issue, it coincided with and was a cover for some new massive shipment of men and matériel from the fascist countries. This time, Italy countered Negrin's action with the announcement that ten thousand of its soldiers would be withdrawn and returned to their homeland. It sounded good, but those returned forces turned out to be either part of the normal rotation of troops or soldiers who were wounded or ill. There was still the same Italian fighting force left in Spain.

What motivated President Negrin to propose the withdrawal of the Internationals? The Republican army was now a relatively cohesive, trained force, and it did not need the Internationals as shock troops. The influx of new International volunteers was negligible, and the ranks of those who had come earlier had been decimated by casualties. The last group from the United States had arrived in June of 1938. What few volunteers came were just trickling in over the border, for the recruiting organization in Paris was no longer functioning. The lack of replacements and continuing casualties meant that the International Brigades became composed mostly of Spaniards. Even the Lincoln Battalion was three-fourths Spanish, and the 15th Brigade (English speaking) was led by a Spanish major. The *Volunteer for Liberty*, the internal publication of the American volunteers, was published partly in Spanish.

Finally, Negrin wanted to protect the Internationals, who would certainly be in immediate and tremendous danger if captured by the victorious Franco forces. Negrin's offer combined with Franco's refusal demonstrated clearly to the world the volunteer nature of the Republic's Internationals, and also showed the organized, government-sponsored nature of the participation of German and Italian troops on the other side. The government hoped that the action would end the pretense, supported by Lord Halifax of England and other European politicians, that both sides were equal in numbers of foreign troops. It was also hoped that the returning Brigaders would be valuable in developing support for the Republic in their homelands.

Tragically, Negrin's action did not lead the League to lift its nonintervention policies, nor did President Roosevelt, still under pressure from the political right and the Catholic hierarchy of the United States, cancel the American arms embargo.

On October 4, 1938, the withdrawal was announced officially in the Republic. A team of eleven observers from the League came to supervise our removal. Negrin's proposal was so complete, so sweeping, that even those who had been granted Spanish citizenship since the beginning of the war (July 5, 1936) were to be sent out. The breadth of the Republic's ruling meant that even those who had come from the prison camps of the Nazis or fascists, or from countries with dictatorships, would be forced to leave. These men were devastated. They had offered their lives to fight fascism, many in the hope of finding a safe new home in Spain, and now they, too, would be sent away. Some had adopted Spanish citizenship, married Spanish women, and started families. Now their dream of a safe haven was gone, taken from them by the very forces to whom they had entrusted their lives. Ultimately, they would walk over the border into concentration camps in southern France that were little more than barbed-wire-enclosed compounds, where meals consisted of some bread laid out on the ground and where sanitation was minimal and disease widespread.

The official count of the commission was that there were 12,673 "foreigners" (including medical and other noncombatants) still in Spain, The best estimate is that 59,380 had come offering themselves to the Republic, of whom 9,934, or almost 17 percent, were killed.

Even though rumors of Negrin's action had been circulating for a week or so, and there had been vague talk of such an action for some months, when the news actually reached us it was stunning. At the moment of Negrin's announcement, most of the I.B. were at the front in the Sierra Pandols under intense pressure from rebel attack. With this news, of course, their central concern became survival until they could be repatriated. None wanted to be killed or wounded in the last days of fighting, especially after they had been declared dispensable. Still, many were wounded, captured, or killed in the last few hours of our participation in the war.

Psychologically, it was the worst of times. Everyone wanted to get out, but all hell had broken loose along the front. September 23, 1938, was the last day the Lincolns were officially in action. But it took more than an official order to get the Brigaders out. Some were surrounded and had to fight their way out, and some had to sneak through enemy lines and swim across the Ebro to safety. Many in those last days didn't make it.

Not being in the front lines, I nevertheless had mixed feelings about our recall. I was keenly aware that we hadn't defeated Franco. But the possibility of going home became more and more attractive, and, as the days went by, the idea took hold and began to dominate my thoughts.

The universally accepted, but unstated, idea had been that the term of enlistment was until the Republic was safe, the fascists defeated. Therefore, there had been no time frame for leaving, no sense of "when" or "until." Now, even though I could understand Negrin's action, I was consumed with guilt and self-doubt. "What went wrong? How had we failed?" At the same time, I felt an exquisite relief for myself that was combined with anger against the insurgents. And I was consumed with rage against the bumblings of the Republic, against Roosevelt for his arms embargo, against the reactionary British and French governments, against Stalin for not doing enough, and, of course, against the fascist nations. Overriding it all were my self-doubts and guilt, wondering whether I had done enough. A few of our Spanish comrades thought we were deserting them, but most proudly felt they were good enough to do without us.

When I heard the announcement of our imminent departure, it became difficult for me to plan any work. I just went on, moment to moment, doing only those lab tests or transfusions that were required. I knew that at any time my life would abruptly change. Life was just "on hold" from that moment forward. In the lab, I began to put everything in order, making lists of things to be done, where things were, where supplies came from, so that whoever took over from me would know where to find things with a minimum of stress and confusion.`

Then one day we were pulled out of all combat, all administrative posts, all medical and technical positions. The wounded in the hospitals were concentrated and moved north as quickly as their physical condition allowed. We were sent to several locations in northern Catalonia up toward the French border. Only a very few Brigaders were left temporarily in Barcelona to tidy the records and finish the few essential administrative jobs. Soon they, too, had to be "counted" for departure. In the last days of fighting, when the Republic's resistance north of Barcelona collapsed, many of the medical personnel and some of their more seriously ill patients were able to cross over, only hours ahead of the moment the fascists seized and sealed the border.

Before the time of Negrin's announcement, the fascists had driven through to the Mediterranean coast just north of Valencia, where the Ebro River empties into the Mediterranean, and had split the Republic in two. There had been a rush to get as many men north as possible. After the last bridges were blown, there were plenty of Brigaders still in the southern half of the country. They were moved east and north and concentrated in the Valencia area.

Evacuation from the south as the rebel forces were threatening to cut through to the Mediterranean was very difficult. After the bridge across the Ebro River near the sea had been bombed, one could look down and see the huge sections that had been torn out of the supports. To get them across, patients were put in a light rail car and men pushed the car over the bridge. Because of the weakness of the structure, it was feared that sending a locomotive across would have led to a collapse. Our *autochir,* which was also south at that moment, had to be abandoned. A day or so later the bridge was bombed again, taking out much of the roadbed, so it could not be crossed, even on foot. This meant that those still south could go north, a few at a time, only in hazardous small-boat trips along the coast at night. These men, many still recovering from their wounds, could never be sure of making it out of the country until they had actually landed in Republican territory.

I was sent to an encampment just outside the small city of Ripoll, about sixty-five miles due north of Barcelona, closer to France. We were a mixed group of a combatants together with many medical and administrative personnel. News was sparse; rumors were plentiful. The only thing I remember positively is eating raw turnips out of the fields, a vegetable I hate when cooked. Turnips and impatience symbolize those days for me. We listened to the radio and read whatever newspaper accounts we could find of the fighting and of the political machinations both inside Spain and out. In a peculiar sense, the war had become somewhat remote.

Then we were officially discharged from the army, but only some of us had our passports returned. Most of those who didn't get theirs back felt that their documents had been turned over to the Comintern for use in planting men in various countries. We were outfitted in civilian clothes. The whole experience of waiting seemed unreal. Our prolonged stay in Ripoll, we found out later, was in large part due to the French government's being very slow in granting us clearance to enter, and also because it insisted that all of the costs of our transportation be paid in advance. This took time to arrange.

While we were waiting in Ripoll for our departure, a parade and farewell to the International Brigades was held on the streets of Barcelona. It was an emotional good-bye. The top governmental and political leaders made speeches—many, many speeches—to thank the Brigaders for their help and to wish them well. But the real salute came from the people who crowded the streets, showered the Brigaders with flowers, and wept their own good-bye—weeping that undoubtedly reflected their understanding that the departure of the Internationals signified that their cause was all but lost.

But we up at Ripoll didn't have such an event to punctuate the end of the war and give us a sense of completion. We simply sat there as if in a suspended state. We kept asking questions, denying the reality of what was happening militarily: Why were we leaving before the war was won or lost? Waiting here with nothing to do, with no sense of mission, made us think over and over again about our time here. It reinforced our conflicting emotions of the anticipation of seeing our homes again and of guilt for leaving before finishing the job. Our thoughts repeated themselves over and over, as we struggled with our feelings of boredom, of anxiety, and even of anger.

With the fascists on the move northward, we were fearful, too, that we might not get out in time to avoid capture, or worse. We had many discussions about hiking across the Pyrenees once again, this time back to France. We wondered how we would find our way without the French guides who had so carefully brought us across. How could we avoid the patrols? How could we keep from falling to our deaths? I had crossed in July, but this was winter and the passes would be filled with snow. And what would we do once we crossed the border? Question after question, all in an attempt to give some substance to the confusion and emptiness we were living with.

As I waited through the long days for our departure, it seemed time for me to assess what had happened, what the International Brigades had contributed, what was leading to Franco's victory, what it was that I had volunteered for. While I had very mixed feelings about not having been in the lines, I felt satisfied with the work that I had done in the medical service, satisfied that I had helped to rescue the wounded and save lives.

The organization of the traveling lab and transfusion service had definitely been a contribution.

Throughout the war, the Brigades had been placed on the most active fronts, where the insurgents were striking the hardest. Initially they had gone into the lines without training or organization, and in the early period the number of our men who were captured, missing in action, wounded, or killed was extremely high. Essentially, what we had contributed most in our battles was to help hold back the enemy in order to create a breathing spell during which the Republic could solve some of its internal problems.

The Republic had needed time to create and train a disciplined army, and space to recover from its political mistakes. We'd helped to give them that time. The presence of the I.B. had also generated a great deal of international support, both politically and financially, and had given courage and hope to many Spaniards that at least some of the world was with them. And not unimportant was the effective medical support that came with the Internationals.

Now we were facing the reality of a Franco victory. The reasons for defeat were many. It was difficult to know them all, but certainly the two biggest factors were the refusal of other governments to sell and deliver munitions and other supplies to the Republic, and the fact that, on the Franco side, there had been continuous and massive deliveries of men, armaments, and supplies from fascist nations.

My feelings about the Spanish people had become so different. While the people of Spain had been going through the years of war with very limited resources and had suffered material deprivation, they had achieved a freedom and sense of self-respect that was never theirs before. I had learned to like them and their land. Maybe it was in part the sense of responsibility one has for a person whose life one has tried to save. Most of all, I had also learned, in a most profound way, to respect the people of Spain. They made do with so little and did so much with what little they had. They evidenced an innate courtesy, warmth, and friendliness toward us that did not permit of anything but friendship in return. The Spaniards I had met were so distant from my preconceptions of a people about whom I had known only little, from reading or watching movies.

As I waited to leave Spain, I began to think of going back to school, of planning for a future, of intimate sharing with a woman. I wondered what it would be like to live without unconsciously sweeping the sky, to listen without fear to the sound of a plane, not to duck when a car back-fired. Should I go back to UCLA and return to my premed classes? Would I really be happier as a bacteriology major? How could I continue the fight against fascism that I had started here? Could I combine the two, the struggle for democracy and an academic or professional career? Was the Depression deepening, or were things getting better? Could I really help change and improve my country? If so, how could I do that? And what about my old wish to be a novelist? Was that gone for good?

In my evaluation, somehow the role of the Communist party wasn't much of a factor. The party was just there, doing its job, and, as far as I could see, doing a good job. The squabbles about leadership, how the various high-level political commissars had done their jobs in Spain hadn't really touched me. I had heard of the arguments, especially about individual commissars on top, but there wasn't any direct connection with my life or work. The party's key role in the International Brigades somehow didn't make itself felt overtly, not, at least, in the medical service, certainly not at my level. I had joined the Spanish party somewhere along the line, but I don't remember attending any meetings. It was just something American party members and YCLers did. My membership card had a picture of me wearing my heavy, knitted, gray wool scarf, the one that so often had lice. But as I was assessing what had happened, the role of party was not a very important part of my thinking. It was just a given in my thoughts, a necessary part of the struggle against fascism.

As we were going home, the cliché "they have not died in vain" kept running around in my mind. Was it true? To what purpose had so many given their lives, had I offered mine? The war in Spain was nearly lost. In fact, in the short space of three and a half months, it would end.

Under the circumstances, it was hard to believe that my comrades had not died in vain. Yet I also knew that the battle in Spain had been necessary and worthwhile, that the struggle for decency in the world would and must continue. If we had not defeated fascism, we had at least demonstrated a will to resist. I knew, too, that after taking a short time to draw a fresh breath, I would be a part of that movement, even if I could not conceive what form my contribution might take.

So why did I volunteer, why did I go?

There is no easy answer. But one thing is clear. I have never regretted my decision. Quite the contrary! To support what I believed in, to combat forces that stood for everything I considered evil, to have put myself at risk for something other than myself, was, and is, a source of great personal pride. That it was an instantaneous decision was consonant with many of the major decisions later in my life—buying homes, making investments, deciding to get married—all rarely burdened by the regret of hindsight.

I knew that the civilian life I would return to would not be serene, but I was committed to a struggle for a better world. "Antifascist" and "prodemocracy" had become the words that I felt defined me. If I left one battlefield, I would find another on which to continue the fight for a better world. In a real sense, for me the fight in Spain had been more than a fight to save only Spain. I came to see it, as much as anything, as a fight against fascism and a struggle for greater democracy in our own country.

Finally, the morning came for our group to leave. On December 2, 1938, I was given a 6 x 8-½ inch piece of paper, dated Barcelona, 27 de Noviembre de 1938, which I still have, from the Ministerio de Defensa Nacional. On it was the signature of El General Presidente. It read: "Rubin, Henri, combatant of the nationality American forms part of a convoy which has to cross the French frontier." Three hundred and twenty-seven of us marched to the train station in Ripoll, where we listened with limited patience to some farewell speeches from the mayor and others, then climbed into five passenger cars. The small engine huffed and puffed, moving us slowly north, fifteen winding miles through the mountains up to the border town of Puigcerda. There we disembarked, listened to some more farewell speeches from town officials, and then ambled the few hundred yards over the border into France.

The tracks there were not equipped with a turntable, and so as soon as we had detrained, the train that had brought us started backing down the line toward Ripoll. Luckily, we had arrived a bit early, for, precisely at noon, our scheduled arrival time, two squadrons of enemy planes appeared to strafe and bomb the station. The people of Puigcerda, who had come to wish us farewell, fortunately had gone back to their homes or businesses, so there were no casualties among them. The train, too, was undamaged, as it had already disappeared around the bend to the south. But it was clear that enemy intelligence was well informed about our troop movements; only their timing was off.

I watched all this from the French side with a sense of fear and disbelief. My fear was the routine reaction to bombing. The disbelief was that this could no longer harm me; I was now just a spectator. The attack, I am sure, reflected the anger the fascists felt over the International Brigades, who had prevented them from achieving the early victory they had expected. At that moment, we were officially noncombatants, not even in their country, and certainly no longer any threat.

In France, we were immediately surrounded by the French national police, who had been awaiting our arrival. We were also carefully counted by the League of Nations commission. The French government was apparently fearful that we were carrying some sort of virus that might contaminate the local population with a dangerous communist, antigovernment ideology. Perhaps, too, they feared that those of us who had no safe homeland to return to would try to melt away and hide in neutral France. Interestingly, although the guards' mission was to contain us, many of them quietly signaled their sympathy for our cause by smiles, winks, or waves when their officers weren't looking.

While we waited for the train to take us north to our ship, the locals of the little village of Bourg-Madame fed us. How they fed us! Baguettes actually baked fresh that same morning with real butter. The crust crackled when I tore the loaf apart. The smell of yeast was appetite-tingling. And fresh scrambled eggs gloriously cooked in butter, not olive oil. And milk, yes, fresh milk! We didn't talk much; we mostly stuffed ourselves and grinned at each other. There was nothing to say that our happy faces weren't already expressing.

Fred Thompson of the Friends of the Abraham Lincoln Brigade, who had come from the States to escort us back home, gave each of us, among other things, a pack of Galouise, that incredibly strong and coarse brand of cigarette that is so popular in France. After our wonderful meal, while strolling about, waiting for our train, one of the comrades lit a cigarette, and, in a gesture to signify that the time of rationing and hardship was over, took one puff and flipped the cigarette into a corner of the small station.

I watched, a momentary sense of horror and disbelief flooding over me as I thought about how carefully we had horded our tobacco. On the rare occasions when we got a real cigarette, we often cut it in two and rerolled the parts to make two cigarettes. At the very least we saved the cigarette butts. But after that initial moment of shock, one by one, as if by compulsion, each of us followed our profligate comrade's example. We lit a cigarette, took one puff, and symbolically threw it down next to his, until there was a pile of smoldering cigarettes that seemed huge. Later that day, as the train sped north and when my pack was empty, I halfway regretted having been so cavalier. But what a glorious, liberating feeling it was to be able to throw that cigarette away with such disdain. It was a reminder, too, that almost a year before, in a letter dated January 10, 1938, to a UCLA friend, I had added a postscript: "When I come back to UCLA, I'm not going to mingle with people but shall merely sit on the library steps, eating bar after bar of chocolate, and smoke cigarettes, throwing the butts away."

The train sped north to Toulouse, where our three cars were hooked onto the Toulouse-Paris express. When it stopped, the Red Cross tried to hand us bread and cheese, but the guards kept them away. During our very brief stay in Paris, we were shunted to some out-of-the-way station and surrounded by armed guards, once again so that no demonstrations of solidarity could be mounted by any sympathizers. Our cars were then attached to a train going west. When we reached the Atlantic Ocean at Cherbourg, our group was put into buses and quickly transported to a camp heavily enclosed with barbed wire. In the recent past, it had been the French equivalent of our Ellis Island.

We remained there for several days, stranded because the maritime workers were on strike and would man no ships. A few of the guys slipped through the barbed wire at night and went into town, but most of us didn't think it worthwhile. We had no French francs, we didn't speak French, we were being fed, we didn't want prostitutes. We were so near home that a sort of lassitude hit most of us. The conditions in the camp weren't bad. We had cots and blankets, and the food was satisfactory, even if not three-star cuisine. After a proposal by one of the French officials that they would take us back home immediately if we would agree to go on a nonunion ship, by unanimous vote we made our position clear. No matter how much we wanted to get home, we would not scab on the strikers, we would not be strikebreakers. After a few days, the union, in a gesture of respect for us and in solidarity with the Spanish Republic, gave special dispensation and authorized the manning of a ship that would take us to New York.

In addition to the returning Brigaders, the ship, *The City of Paris*, also had its normal complement of paying passengers. My memories of that trip aboard the ship are hazy, except for the food. Each morning I went in for breakfast at the beginning of the first seating. My order to the waiter was gargantuan: I ordered virtually everything offered. Halfway through the meal, the richness of the food would overcome me and I would have to run to the toilet to vomit. But so great was my psychological hunger that, immediately after rinsing my mouth and washing my face, I returned to the table and began anew.

For months after I got home, my appetite seemed to know no bounds, although my digestive system continued to have trouble handling what was available. And no one who has not experienced extended sieges of diarrhea and dysentery can appreciate the acute relief and pleasure of not having to worry about soiling one's underwear.

We landed in New York, where grim-faced FBI agents looked us over, memorizing our faces, for we had been labeled "premature antifascists." Premature antifascists meant that we were not just soldiers, or soldiers of fortune, but, more dangerously, "antifascists." To the government, we were fighters who threatened the peace of the nation. The passports of those of us who had them were confiscated and never returned. Those who hadn't gotten theirs back in Spain had trouble establishing that they were really U.S. citizens and had the right to enter their own country.

Not much later, on December 23, I read with dismay that Franco was throwing 350,000 rebel troops against the Republican forces in the province of Catalonia. They were resisted by 120,000 soldiers who were outgunned fifteen to one in aviation, thirty to one in tanks, ten to one in small arms and automatic weapons, and twenty to one in light artillery. The Republican forces had no heavy artillery at all. As they fell back, they had only thirty-seven thousand rifles, little ammunition, and nothing else. In Barcelona, there were a million refugees. These outgunned and out-manned forces formed a human shield for the more than four hundred thousand civilian refugees who streamed north across the border, braving the heights of the Pyrenees, the cold, and the snow. At that moment, on French soil were ten thousand machine guns, twenty-four torpedo boats, four hundred aircraft, as well as rifle ammunition and artillery shells that the legitimate government of Spain had bought and paid for from the Soviet Union, Czechoslovakia, Mexico, and a few other countries. All of that matériel had been denied to the Republic, an act given legitimacy by the Non-Intervention Pact.

The Republican government fell on April 1, 1939. Immediately, the Vatican sent Franco a telegram thanking him for a "Christian victory."

Resistance in Spain continued on a sporadic basis because of the fear of reprisals. The Franco government publicly claimed that there were two million persons who had to be punished under the "Law of Political Responsibility." Somewhere between two and four hundred thousand were executed after the war, and two million or more people were sent to labor camps. In France, Pétain agreed to hand over German refugees to the Gestapo. The Spanish church was given exclusive control over education in the postwar state. Fascism, dominant in much of Europe, was pushing to extend its control.

Six months later Hitler marched into Poland, and the war the world had feared began in earnest.

CHAPTER
11

Epilogue

For years afterward, most of the vets had trouble getting passports. Even later, with honorable discharges from the U.S. Army for service in World War II, we were not allowed the luxury of travel outside the United States. It took many federal court battles and much political pressure to reverse this policy. It was seventeen years before I even considered applying for a passport.

In 1965, when I wanted to visit Europe with my wife, Lillian, I filled out the application for a passport months ahead of the start of our projected trip, fully expecting that I would have to go to court to force the government to issue it. I was surprised when my passport arrived in a few days without a fight. Apparently, enough of my fellow vets had fought the battle before me.

We were pariahs to our government. When Brigaders volunteered for the armed forces in World War II, the official army line, at first, was that we were not to be sent outside of the continental limits, so that we would not have contact with European communists. This ruling was later successfully challenged. Even so, most of us were sent to the Pacific combat zone. But despite all of the government's fears about our politics, some of the Brigaders, because of their experience and skills, were needed for the war effort. Some, therefore, were sent across the Atlantic to assignments behind the German and Italian lines to work with the various resistance forces, which, ironically, were often communist or communist-led.

More than six hundred American vets served in World War II, in addition to another three hundred more in the merchant marine. In all, about twenty-five Spanish vets gave their lives for their country in World War II. Many were decorated for bravery. Between sixty and seventy, including myself, were commissioned as officers. As a side note, many Spaniards-in-exile volunteered to fight with the French, and when the tanks of the Free French entered Paris for its liberation from the Germans, many were manned by Spanish personnel, and three tank turrets proudly carried the names of Spanish battles—Madrid, Teruel, or Jarama—painted on their sides.

In New York, some of the returned vets formed the Veterans of the Abraham Lincoln Brigade, which had become the blanket name for all of us who had served in Spain, no matter in which battalion or whether in combat or not. Then posts were formed in Los Angeles, San Francisco, and elsewhere. It was not just a self-help organization or a vehicle to remind the world and ourselves that we were heroes. Yes, we helped fellow vets and made people remember the war. Yes, we sent help to those Spaniards who had fled across the border into France, and we helped, as best we could, those continuing the fight against Franco. But at all times, it has been a political organization—raising the banner against fascism, supporting our country in its war against fascism, and later helping the people of Central America, who were suffering under their own dictatorships.

Of the roughly thirty-three hundred Americans who went to Spain, about eight hundred are known to have died. Over a hundred prisoners of war were not repatriated until months after the end of fighting. The frightening mortality figures that Rep had given me that April noon at UCLA were much worse than the reality. Still, of those who had been combatants and survived, a majority had been wounded at least once.

In Spain, I had lost track of that mixed group of five with whom I had boarded the bus in Los Angeles. But as I was leaving the country, I found out that Hera and Mark had been killed in action. John was missing in action and was never found, and Al had lost a leg and had been sent home. My friend Sig, too, had died on the battlefield. My liver had saved my life. I was the only physically unscarred survivor of our Los Angeles cohort.

We who came back were still young in years, but both bodies and minds had lost their youthful innocence. There was no severance pay, other than a Greyhound bus ticket back to our homes and twenty-five dollars for food along the way. The Friends of the Abraham Lincoln Brigade raised money for medical care for those of us needing extended treatment. Many sympathetic doctors and dentists in cities across the country volunteered their services. For me, it meant that the root of my broken molar was finally removed and a bridge made to take its place. For most of us, it was a quiet return without celebration. We came back to a nation that was still in the midst of the Depression. Sixteen million people were unemployed and jobs were hard to find.

I returned to Los Angeles to a warm and relieved welcome from my family, who could never understand why I had gone. Although my father didn't know what to make of me, I was his only son, the only one who could carry on the family name. So he was greatly relieved that I was alive. But I was unrepentant and had not given up my radical ideas. So he was, as always, disappointed. He suggested again that his insurance agency would be a good place for me to begin the return to normal life. But even as he said the words, he knew how far apart we were, how impossible it was for us to understand each other.

At first, I briefly considered volunteering to work with Dr. Norman Bethune in China, where he was introducing the same blood-transfusion system that I had used in Spain. I was interested in the Chinese revolution and welcomed the idea of joining the communist forces fighting against Chiang Kai-shek. My safe passage through the months of war had reinforced both my youthful sense of invulnerability as well as my political commitment.

As I thought about a China stint, I wondered what I could take with me that would make my life more comfortable there. Apart from a few technical items, such as a supply of good transfusion needles, I finally came up with two items: a large supply of saccharine to satisfy my sweet tooth and, remembering the wartime dullness of the diet in Spain, dehydrated onions to give flavor to what I suspected would be a very thin, bland diet. But China never materialized in my life. No one was recruiting very hard, nor could I find anyone who knew how to get there.

I reenrolled at UCLA, where I found that I had become quite a campus curiosity. The pacifists looked upon me as a sort of antediluvian adventurer, the Left saw me as a hero worthy of respect. The majority on campus were pro-Loyalist, and their positive response reflected those sympathies. Naturally, I loved being the center of attention. The combination of being center-stage, combined with the difficulty of readjustment to civilian life, particularly to student life, made studying very difficult, and my grades began to reflect that fact. To be a successful premedical student requires continued, hard study, which was practically impossible for me at that time. Then a combination of Franco's success and the immediate horror of Hitler's invasion of Poland moved the Spanish combat from center stage.

At UCLA, besides attending to my studies, I also arranged for an exhibit of contemporary (meaning wartime) Spanish art—paintings and ink sketches from the brush and pen of Sim, a Catalonian artist, and Bardsano, a Basque painter who depicted in somber tones pictures of fascist cruelty, the early days of the war, and violent scenes of street fighting.

I spent time with the Young Communist League and there met Jean, the leader of the campus club. We became comrades and fell in love. I like to think that it was my sterling character and sex appeal that she responded to, but I know that my status as a Spanish vet gave me a glamour that didn't hurt my courtship of her.

In spite of the fact that she was "sort of engaged" to Bob, a close friend of mine who was then studying at UC Berkeley, our relationship became serious and we decided to marry.

Since we thought of a wedding as a bourgeois ceremony, we decided to elope and present our families with a fait accompli. Our friends Jack and Miriam drove us to Ventura, about ninety miles north of Los Angeles. We chose Ventura because it was in a different county and, therefore, wedding announcements there wouldn't be published in the Los Angeles papers.

The county offices were in a massive building where, after paying two dollars for our license, we were directed to a justice of the peace. In a small, marble room he mumbled his way through the ceremony, reading the words from a well-thumbed book. When he came to the part "and with this ring I do thee wed," Jack handed me a ring, knowing that I would not have bought one, thinking it too bourgeois. He'd brought one that he had gotten as a free prize in a Cracker Jack box. Afterward, I asked the judge what I owed.

"Whatever it's worth."

With embarrassment I mumbled, "It's worth a lot more, but we're sort of broke," and I handed him three well-folded singles. Leaving his chamber, I saw him vainly trying to separate the bills into more than three. Outside, in the hall, I grabbed for Jean's hand to get the ring off, but she pulled away and gave a shriek that was heard down the long, marble-lined corridor. Heads popped out of doors to see what was wrong. Embarrassed, we went quickly into the nearest stairwell to get out of the building.

Neither her father nor my parents reacted favorably to a mixed-religion marriage. Her father, who traced his family to the Mayflower, was polite to me but privately lamented to Jean that "he never expected his family to become a melting pot." My family was equally polite to Jean, but when he heard the news, my father could only ask, "Did you have to?" He refused to refer to my marriage again. Mother kept after me, too, with little digs about Jean, wanting to know if our children would be raised as Jews and how we would resolve religious and cultural differences.

My transition to civilian life had begun in earnest.

Index

Sanidad Militar, 107
sanitation, 85–86
Saxton, Reginald (Reggie), 111, 116
Servicio Sanitario (35th Division), 101, 137
Set Cases, 58
sexuality, 134–36
Sigmund (Sig) (volunteer), 31–33, 35, 40, 48, 153
Sim, 155
Soccoro Rojo (Red Aid), 107
socialism, 18
Social Security, 18
Soviet Union, 18, 67, 150
Soviet volunteers, 70
Spain (see also Republic of Spain): anti-Semitism of, 19; armies, 38–39; caste system, 64, 82; Cortes (parliament), 20, 21, 64; division between church and state, 5; history of, 19, 139; unions, 39–40, 82
Spanish Aid Committee, 107
Spanish Army of Africa, 38–39
Spanish Battalion, 72
SS *Bremen*, 5
Stalin, Joseph, 17, 18, 70
Statue of Liberty, 31
Steffan, Jonna, 91–92
Steffan, Pedro, 91–92
Steinbeck, John, 7
stretcher bearers, 105, 129
Switzerland, 69

Tarazona de la Mancha, 73
Ted (doctor), 128
Teruel, battle of, 116–18
Texaco Company, 39
Thaelmann Brigade, 71–72
Third International (Comintern), 39–40
35th Division Medical Services, 101, 137
Thompson, Fred, 148
Tito, 69
Togliatti, Palmiro, 39
transfusions, 107–9, 124, 126–27

triage system, 109–11, 124
Tueda, 106

unions, 8; and evacuation, 149; French, 40; Spanish, 39–40, 82
United Front against Fascism, 39, 40
United States: anti-Nazi sentiment, 5; anti-Semitism in, 16; arms embargo, 67; fascist organizations in, 16; isolationist position of, 4; support for Franco, 39
University of California at Los Angeles (UCLA), 10

Vatican (see also Catholic Church), 150
venereal disease, 135–36
Veterans of the Abraham Lincoln Brigade, 153
Victor (medical worker), 116
Volunteer for Liberty, 140
volunteers, 26–27; attempts at discretion, 30, 31–32; bickering among, 51–53; issue of supplies to, 70–71; and mail, 81–82; nationalities of, 48, 51, 60–61, 68–72; payment of, 25, 85; security issues, 29; silence, commitment to, 5–6, 21–22, 24, 31, 32, 37, 42, 48; songs, 79–80; unprovoked attacks on, 49–51, 147–48

Webb, 3
Wehrmacht, 66–67
wines, 112
women, status of, 66
worker organizations, 39
Worker's Olympiad, 68
World War I, 13
World War II, 84, 152–53

Yiddish, 44–45, 91
Young Communist League (YCL), 17, 18–19, 155

Zamora, Alacalá, 20, 21
Zionist Club, 13
Zionist movement, 17

HANK RUBIN, born in 1916, was a student at UCLA before enlisting as an international brigadist in the Spanish Civil War where he served as a machine gunner, blood transfusionist, and laboratory techinician. His next round of military service included a stint as a 1st Lieutenant in the Medical Administrative Corps in World War II. In civilian life, he has worked as a restaurateur, food technologist, food and wine columnist, and high school teacher. He lives with his wife, Lillian, in San Francisco.